The Attuned Family

✦

How To Be a Great Parent To Your Kids and a Great Lover To Your Spouse

Keith Witt, Ph.D.

Santa Barbara Graduate Institute Publishing
iUniverse, Inc.
New York Lincoln Shanghai

The Attuned Family
How To Be a Great Parent To Your Kids and a Great Lover To Your Spouse

iUniverse books may be ordered through booksellers or by contacting:

iUniverse
2021 Pine Lake Road, Suite 100
Lincoln, NE 68512
www.iuniverse.com
1-800-Authors (1-800-288-4677)

The information, ideas, and suggestions in this book are not intended as a substitute for professional advice. Before following any suggestions contained in this book, you should consult your personal physician or mental health professional. Neither the author nor the publisher shall be liable or responsible for any loss or damage allegedly arising as a consequence of your use or application of any information or suggestions in this book.

ISBN: 978-0-595-43846-4 (pbk)
ISBN: 978-0-595-88171-0 (ebk)

Printed in the United States of America

Contents

Introduction

An attuned family has parents who attend with acceptance to what they are feeling, thinking, and wanting, reach with acceptance for what their children and partner are feeling, thinking, and wanting, and then organize their thinking and behavior to serve love and health.

Imagine today is the last day of your life. You are on your deathbed. You are comfortable, lucid, at peace with your impending passage, and are reflecting back on your personal history.

What is the story of your life? As you matured, were you increasingly true to your principles? Did you learn to understand, accept, and love yourself better? Were you progressively better at giving and receiving love with your spouse, children, family, friends, and associates? Did you grow in your understanding and ability to be a great lover to your spouse? Did you grow in your ability to be a great parent to your children?

If the answer to any of the above questions is "no," what would you give for a chance to change your story? Imagine how wonderful it would be to have the time and opportunity to better love yourself and others.

Good news! Today is almost certainly not the last day of your life. You probably have years ahead to love and grow. We always have a chance to change our story.

At any given moment we can be more or less healthy physically, psychologically, spiritually, or relationally. People in a healthy moment are usually becoming more accomplished at knowing and loving themselves and others. People in an unhealthy moment are usually allowing themselves to get worse at these things. In an attuned family each parent consciously works at compassionate self-knowledge and loving connection.

How the #%! do I do that?

Many years ago my friend Mark asked me to go down the Rogue River in Oregon with him and a bunch of his river buddies. My river experience was limited to one ecstatic but brief trip down the Stanislaus (a relatively tame river in the

Sierras) when I was in my twenties, but Mark assured me that he and his friends were accomplished white water rafters and it would be a blast.

After driving seven hours Mark and I finally arrived at the put out, had a series of hurried introductions, and I found myself in a boat with four other men paddling into a placid loop of the Rogue River. I had on a helmet and a life vest, and was wielding an unfamiliar paddle. Mark, who was the steersman, gave me about five minutes of instruction on what I was supposed to do (basically paddle forward and backward when he called out directions), but I trusted him and his guys and believed I was ready for anything.

Suddenly we were in the rapids, and I got why they are called rapids. Everything started happening unbelievably fast. We seemed to be hurtling straight down a waterfall of huge boulders and crashing cascades of water at a hundred miles an hour. I crouched down as low as I could in the raft and still be able to dig my paddle into the water, and wondered why they didn't have seatbelts in these things.

I had about a minute of this chaotic thrill ride when one of those transformative events happened; an event that would echo through my life. Mark fell out of the boat.

We were now careening down the rapid with no steersman and Mark clinging to my side of the raft saying, "Pull me in."

I grabbed him ineffectually by his shoulder harness and tugged as hard as I could. He didn't budge.

"Pull me in!" he shouted again, and, feeling intensely ashamed and terrified for my friend, I pulled with all my might, hoping that hysterical strength would levitate Mark back into the relative (very relative) safety of the raft. Again he didn't budge.

Mark was an expert riverman. He immediately got that I had no idea how to pull a man into a raft that was careening down a major rapid, and, knowing he was safer going down the rapid alone than clinging to a raft that might crush him against a rock, he let go and managed to guide himself through the rapids to the next smooth stretch of river.

When we were all reunited Mark explained to me how you have to lean out over the edge of the raft, grab the chest harness of your buddy and lever him over the side into the raft. I practiced it a couple of times and, sure enough, it worked.

Of course, I didn't know this when Mark fell into the river, but I was still intensely ashamed that, through my lack of knowledge and skill, my friend might have been badly hurt, or worse.

In our culture teenagers and adults often enter love affairs or have children without anyone teaching them how to support each other when things get out of control. This can leave people intensely hurt, angry, and ashamed because we often believe we should naturally know what to do in extreme situations. Sometimes we just don't and need a little basic guidance on how to help each other back into the boat.

Attunement is important and desirable in all relationships.

The examples in this book are heterosexual two-parent families, but the principles and practices described apply to single parent families, gay and lesbian families, families with adopted children, families with adult children, families with disabled children or parents, families of all ethnicities, and the countless other constellations of family relationships. Certainly there are unique issues in each of these variations, but it is beyond the scope of this book to deal specifically with them all. Suffice it to say that attunement is possible and desirable, and that each of us can get better at attuning to ourselves, our children, our lovers, and others.

1

We Need Help

Jim is thirty-three, and Sally is thirty-one (Jim and Sally, like all the examples in this book, are conglomerates of people I've known and worked with over the past thirty-three years and forty thousand therapy sessions). They have a little two-year-old boy named Jacob, who is active and demanding. Because they have been fighting with increasing intensity and frequency, Sally called me for therapy. This is their first session.

Jim and Sally appear to be a normal, attractive young middle class couple. Jim is dressed in dark slacks and a white shirt for work, and Sally has loose comfortable pants and a fashionable violet sweatshirt, with no jewelry. Noticing how tired Sally looks and how irritated Jim appears, I immediately start imagining that they have a child under five in the house. I've found that almost all parents of young children suffer from sleep deprivation and increased conflict with each other:

Keith: "So, what brings you here?"

Sally: "We have communication problems." (Jim fidgets uncomfortably as she speaks. Sally appears oblivious to his distress.)

Keith: "What kind of communication problems?"

Sally: "Jim gets mad and hardly ever helps. When I ask him, he thinks I'm being too crabby."

Jim: (The unfairness of this is more than he can handle.) "You're a bitch all the time. Nothing I do pleases you." (Sally winces as he angrily says the word "bitch," but he doesn't appear to notice.)

Keith: "Do you have children under five?"

Sally: (Her eyebrows rise slightly.) "Why yes. We have a two-year-old named Jacob. How did you know?"

Keith: (I'm imagining how hard their lives are right now, and how much pressure they must be putting on themselves and each other to try to do right. The responsibility of a new family in a conflicted marital relationship can be overwhelming.) "You both look sleep deprived and you're not paying much attention to each other as you talk. Sally, you aren't wearing any jewelry and you seem like a woman who enjoys accessories. Little kids, especially little boys, have a tendency to grab for shiny things, so mothers often learn that it's easier to not wear necklaces and earrings."

Both Jim and Sally relax as I talk. They are not consciously aware of it, but having a caring person attune to them is soothing. This attunement involves me attending to and accepting my own sensations, emotions, and thoughts, and then feeling into their experience. As I do this, my conscious purpose is to help them, and my body and brain automatically give dozens of signals through my gaze, facial expression, voice tone and timing, body posture, and content of my speech that supports them feeling "felt" by me. Feeling "felt" by another, caring person is often a sign that he or she is attuning to us:[1]

Sally: (Smiling at me, but unconsciously not including Jim.) "Jake almost ripped my ear off before we went to a potluck last week. I just can't wear my jewelry around him."

Jim: (Angry again at feeling shut out from her warmth as she speaks to me.) "And you let him get away with it. You never punish him when he hurts you. How do you expect him to learn?"

Sally: "Not by yelling at him and scaring him like you do. He's just a little boy."

Jim: "You let him get away with anything. At least I tell him 'no' once in awhile."

Sally: "You're always telling him 'no.' You're mean to him and to me."

Jim: (He looks away in exasperation and falls into sullen silence.) "Sure, whatever."

Keith: (I want to introduce the idea that Jacob has a worldview that is radically different from theirs and is rapidly changing.) "How many months old is Jacob?"

Sally: (Curious.) "He'll be three in June, so I guess he's thirty-two months old. Why do you ask?"

Keith: (I love it when my clients ask questions. Asking a question can open you up to new perspectives.) "There are differences in how a child thinks, feels, relates to parents, and behaves between twenty-four and thirty-two months. Doesn't Jake have better language skills than he did at two? A two-year-old usually knows about fifty words, while a three-year-old knows around a thousand.[2] Have you noticed him having any unusual fears in the last few months?"

Jim: (He is an electrical engineer and his scientist self is hooked by hard data.) "He just started saying that there are monsters in the closet. Does that mean he has a problem?"

Keith: "Probably not. As children's capacity for thought increases, as their brains grow, they have to process things like the dream images they have just as they're waking or after briefly going to sleep. From a little after one to around four, children have a predominantly magical worldview where they can experience dreams or imagined images as real. Kids live in different universes than you and me. For instance, Jacob probably thinks that you both have God-like powers and can do anything."[3]

Sally: (Laughing.) "You're right. He told me to make the sun come up last night at three A.M. I told him I couldn't do that and he got furious."

Jim: (Contemptuously.) "And you let him scream and keep you up for an hour. I just would have told him to be quiet and go back to sleep." (Sally glares angrily at Jim who appears to not notice.)

I've seen enough to have an idea about how parenting Jake is stressing them. I want to examine their relationship with each other, so I shift the focus of the session:

Keith: "How's your sex life." (They both laugh shortly.)

Jim: "What sex life?"

Sally: "Who has time for a sex life?"

Keith: "When's the last time you made love?" (They finally look at each other and something vaguely affectionate seems to pass between them.)

Sally: "When was it, Jim? That night in November when your mother took Jake so we could go to your college reunion?"

Jim: (Smiles.) "That was a fun night."

In this last exchange, Jim and Sally are having a mutually attuned moment. Both are in touch with a nostalgic sense of their previous romantic life. They are remembering their fun evening in November, and are feeling the other resonating with their experience. They're compassionately connected with their own inner experience and empathetically connected with the other's experience. Each feels "felt" by the other, and there is a sense of shared positive intent. Unfortunately, the moment quickly passes, and they snap into their stress-and-fatigue driven defensive patterns:

Sally: "Your mother said that Jacob cried all night."

Jim: (Disgustedly.) "She always exaggerates, and so do you when it comes to poor delicate little Jacob." (This is too much for Sally who tears up and turns hopelessly away from him.)

Sally and Jim are not clear at this moment what their responsibilities are. I believe that they each have a responsibility to be caring to themselves, each other, and Jacob to support their family. I want to help them desire the knowledge and self-discipline to attune to each other and Jacob.

They've shown me a general idea of how they get lost in their pain. I'm sure they have many more individual and relational defensive systems, but it's time to get oriented to who they are, how deeply embedded are their defenses against insight and change, and what are their histories of learning to care for themselves and others:

Keith: "I'd like to ask you some questions about your history. I can see that it's hard to talk about these things without getting plugged into conflict. It's also clear that you'd much rather be loving each other than attacking and hurting." (Once again, in the presence of my attunement, they both relax.)

Sally: "OK."

Jim: "Sure, ask whatever you'd like."

Over the next hour we explore who Sally and Jim are, what their family lives have been since birth, and how they learned to care for themselves and others.

Jim's mother could collapse into terrifying rage when she felt stressed or overwhelmed. She loved babies, but Jim as a toddler became the occasional object of her attacks, usually followed by guilty and tearful attempts at reconciliation. He learned to stoically block out other people emotionally unless he surpassed his tolerance for negative arousal. When his window of tolerance was exceeded, he would feel intense shame, humiliation, and rage, and could lash out at whomever he blamed. As a child this would be his parents or his younger sister (who fought with Jim and acted out rebelliously against some family rules). Now, when Jim felt overwhelmed, he often verbally attacked Sally or Jacob. Growing up, Jim had a strong sense of right and wrong, was quick to make moral judgments, and found other's contempt intolerable. This moral self-righteousness was still a core feature of his personality. On the other hand, as an electrical engineer and a dedicated scientist, Jim respected facts and data.

Meeting Sally at twenty-seven was like a dream come true. Jim's two previous relationships had ended badly. His college sweetheart cheated on him with one of his good friends, and he broke up immediately, even though she begged him to take her back. His next lover was another graduate engineering student who took a post-doctoral fellowship in Boston, leaving Jim devastated. Sally seemed different from other women. She was happy, sexy, and carefree. They laughed, played, and made love daily for two years. When they married Jim believed that he would never feel lonely or deprived again. This changed quickly after marriage. Sally became much less interested in sex, leading Jim to pursue and coerce her. Not surprisingly, this just resulted in her being less close, warm, and emotionally available.

When Sally got pregnant, she became obsessed with being a good mother, eating the right foods and supplements, and having the "right" birth experience. Jim tried manfully to participate but felt increasingly left out. This sense of isolation accelerated after the birth, since Sally believed she had superior knowledge and judgment about parenting, relationships, and childcare, and seemed to pay very little attention to Jim's opinions. Jim adored Jacob but found himself jealous of all the cuddling, warmth, and affection Jacob received from Sally, and disgusted with how she seemed to never say "no" and always let herself be manipulated by Jake (and sometimes her friends). He tried to make up for it by being stricter with Jacob, especially when he felt that Sally was being "controlled" by Jacob's demands. Sally never supported these efforts. They seemed harsh to her, and she felt she had to protect Jacob from Jim's anger. Jim liked to surf and play music with his friends but, between work and family responsibilities, found little time for either.

Sally's parents had a pretty good sense of themselves and their children. Although emotions weren't easily discussed in her family, both parents idolized each other and attuned naturally to Sally and her two older brothers (Sam was three years older, and Ryan was four years older). Life was pretty idyllic in their household until their father died tragically in a car crash when Sally was five. Her mother proceeded to collapse into a severe depression, and Sally and her brothers were emotionally on their own for the next several years. Her mother remarried when Sally was ten, but Sally never got along with her stepfather. He seemed critical and strict to her and competed with her for her mother's attention.

Brother Sam approached her sexually when he was thirteen and she was ten, and they had a secret sexual relationship for several months. Both felt guilty and ashamed of this, and Sam eventually insisted that they stop. Neither ever talked to anyone else about it until Sally told Jim a year after they were married (about the time that she and Jim began to have fights about her apparent disinterest in sex). Jim steadfastly blamed this "molest" (Jim's designation) for her sexual indifference, and thereafter refused to visit Sam and his family.

Since mid-adolescence Sally had a pattern of passionate affiliation with lovers, and then, after one or two years, loss of romantic and erotic interest. Two of her previous lovers had affairs and left her. When she met Jim, there was something special about how solid and steady he was.

Sally took yoga classes when she could (not many since Jacob's birth), saw a chiropractor and a naturopathic healer, and was enormously distressed about the twenty pounds she had put on since pregnancy. She used to work out, but somehow couldn't do it consistently as a mother. In spite of the fact that she was radiant and beautiful when she was relaxed and happy, Sally felt unattractive since Jacob's birth. She ate chocolate cherries as comfort food and felt guilty afterwards.

Both Sally and Jim drank socially; rarely to excess. Both used pot and other drugs in college, and Jim still smoked pot occasionally with his music and surfing buddies, but mostly their partying days were in the past.

Jim was raised Catholic but was now contemptuous of organized religion. Sally believed that spirit permeated and guided everyone's life, and that God communicates in mysterious ways. When she found an owl feather on her windshield the night after she called about counseling, she believed it was a sign that they were on the right path.

Jim and Sally had received very little direct, conscious instruction on how to know themselves emotionally and how to successfully create and maintain healthy internal and interpersonal attunements.

Jim was an intensely masculine individual who was attracted to feminine radiance, loved being on the edge of death surfing big waves and watching sports, and who felt a mission to give his best to his company at work and be a good husband and father at home.

Sally was an intensely feminine person who wanted love in her life and family, could sense balance and imbalance in her relationships, enjoyed making her home a full and pretty place, and valued interpersonal connections.

Neither was much in the habit of self-reflecting what these histories meant to their life or development, or what it meant to be a more masculine or more feminine person. Neither really understood that their worldviews, though similar and connected in myriad ways, were often different in attitudes about love, sex, body, spirituality, meaning, and parenting.

Defensive states, sometimes traits.

Both Jim and Sally had the capacity, when they felt threatened, to enter defensive states of consciousness where they had amplified or numbed emotions, distorted perspectives and thoughts, and destructive impulses. When Jim called Sally a bitch, he was feeling amplified anger, had the distorted perspective that she was mostly uncaring towards him, and was compelled by the destructive impulse to speak harshly. This was an altered state where he had little empathy for the suffering he was causing her, and minimal self-reflection on his own destructive thought and behaviors. Since interpersonal attunement requires compassionate awareness of self and empathetic connection to another, Jim routinely became disconnected when he was threatened. He did not know how to compassionately look within to understand and resolve his defensive states. Instead, he would blame Sally, Jacob or, occasionally, himself (as in "I'm so screwed up, maybe I'm not able to love or worthy of love.").

Defensive states are co-created in early family relationships. Jim learned from his explosive mother to keep to himself and be self-sufficient. On the other hand, if threatened past a certain point, he unconsciously felt he needed to be scarier than the other guy and would get cold and intense. Sally felt, with some justification, that "he was another person" when he was angry. The story he told himself was "I don't let anybody mess with me."

Sally had been a happy baby, the youngest child, and the only girl. These factors predisposed her to be indulged by the rest of the family and not particularly encouraged to be maturely self-reflective when in distressed emotional states. This made it hard to be aware of her own sensations and emotions when Jacob was distressed. A frequent consequence of a parent not noticing her own sensations, emotions, thoughts, and impulses is the tendency to resist setting appropriate boundaries. This can confuse children by allowing them to engage in destructive behaviors. When stressed, Sally tended to indulge Jacob rather than set boundaries, and she became offended rather than emotionally aware when Jim pointed this out.

Sally was unaware of her pattern of becoming sexually distant from her lovers just when the level of intimacy with them began to approximate the depth of connection she had felt with her own father before he was wrenched from her family. Attunement with a man who felt as close as her father restimulated the old trauma of her father's death and her mother's depression, and her sexuality automatically would shut down to provide "safe" separation. The story she told herself about this was that relationships were hot in the beginning and then cooled down. Everybody knew that's the way it was.

Part of Jim and Sally's suffering came from habitual states of consciousness that they had never really examined or considered as blocks to love. Part of their suffering came from sometimes simply not knowing what to do when somebody falls out of the boat.

The power of love.

When my two children, Zoe and Ethan, were little, I used to tell them lots of stories. Children love stories because we humans are driven to make sense of the world, and stories help us do this. Children who are told stories of their own life become more self-aware, verbal, and in touch with their feelings.[4] These stories don't have to be complex. For example, "You got up this morning and came into our room and told me it was raining. You played with Cindy, and I bought both of you ice cream from the store. You cried because I wouldn't buy you the big candy bar, and I told you I understand it's frustrating when you can't have something you want just because it's not good for your body." This story helps the child remember her day, understand and process emotions, and feel "felt" by a parent.

I used to tell my children bedtime stories of magical kingdoms where a girl named Cloe and her brother Nathan had extraordinary adventures. At around nine my son Ethan began to see amazing similarities between Cloe and Nathan and Zoe and Ethan. Often, after one of these stories, Ethan would ask me, "Is there magic in this world?"

This is a tricky question. Children from around one to four years old live in a magical world. They believe they and others can directly control nature and inner experience. An eighteen month old child will call out for her Barbie and believe she is magically creating it when it appears. A twenty month old might be furious at his mother when he feels bad, because she is not magically making him feel better. A two year old will feel deserted if a parent doesn't understand what he is thinking when he points at the street, says "bracks," and wants to visit the train tracks.

Some time after three, children begin to understand that they personally cannot magically make the rain stop, or grandma to appear, but parents apparently can, thus inaugurating a period where children are aware of their own limitations but attribute magical powers to adults. This can last till six or seven when children's brains have developed sufficiently for them to begin to understand the concrete world.[5] Regardless of their worldview, it's always good to give children honest feedback that makes sense to them now, and will still make sense to them in a subsequent developmental stage. In other words, if they remember a message as they develop through childhood, teenage years, young adulthood, adulthood, and parenthood, will it ring true, guide, support, and inspire them in these more mature perspectives? So, how to answer the question, "Is there magic in this world?"

My response to Ethan was always, "Yes, the magic of this world is that we love each other."

The drive to love transcends all human frailty and pathology. We are social creatures and our drive to give and receive love is one of our most fundamental social instincts. Other fundamental instincts are to make meaning of our experience,[6] to establish position on personally important social hierarchies, and to be true to our deepest masculine or feminine essence[7]. The drive to love begins with the infant looking up into mother's eyes (which are drawn irresistibly to her child's) and instinctively mirroring mother's facial expressions, sounds, and inner states. The drive to create attachment to significant parental figures (usually predominantly mother in infancy, but rapidly including father) is hard-wired into our nervous systems.[8]

If a parent can feel into themselves and feel into an infant to provide care that is responsive in a soothing way to the moment-to-moment shifts in the child's physical/emotional/relational states, the infant will probably develop secure attachment. Secure attachment means a child, through reliable access to a caring and responsive caregiver, is supported in developing an influential inner figure of a caring and responsive caregiver. As this sense is created and deepened with consistent attunement, it gradually begins to provide inner direction as to how to interpret and relate to the world. In this sense we tend to parent ourselves the way we were parented.[9]

Another equally valid way of conceptualizing this attachment process is that the parent's nervous system attunes to the child's nervous system to actually guide and help it grow. Current neurobiological research has shown persuasively that a child's brain is literally taught how to grow in relationship with the brains of primary caregivers.[10]

Positive attunement maximizes love and, not surprisingly, maximizes healthy development. John Gottman, one of the preeminent U.S. researchers and clinicians associated with couples and families, suggests that a parent being available and responsive to an infant 30% of the time is all a child needs for healthy development.[11] Other research has demonstrated that the capacity to be non-judgmentally and purposefully self-aware (mindful) is associated with improved immune function, improved cardiovascular health, better relationships, and a general sense of well-being.[12]

As we emerge from adolescence we are attracted to and bond with our sexual reciprocals. If we are a more masculine person, we are drawn to feminine erotic radiance. If we are a more feminine person, we are drawn to masculine presence and depth of consciousness. These attractions create erotic polarities that can progress into love affairs, relationships, marriages, and childbearing. Not surprisingly, our ability to attune to our lover is highly correlated with how secure our attachment style is and involves feeling into ourselves while feeling empathetically into our partner; processes that are also necessary for great parenting. On the other hand, attuning to children and lovers involves related but different sets of knowledge, skills, and principles. Both sets are important to happy families. This is why an attuned family has mothers and fathers who do what it takes to be *both* great parents to their children and great lovers to their spouses.

This book explores attunement from a variety of perspectives and approaches. Not surprisingly, everything presented is influenced and informed by the creative, transformative, and redemptive power of love. This is the magic of this world, that we love each other.

1. Siegal (1999)

2. Cozolino (2002)

3. Wilber (2000)

4. Siegal (2003)

5. Wilber (2000)

6. Kegan (1982)

7. Witt (2005)

8. Siegal (1999)

9. *Ibid*

10. *Ibid*

11. Gottman (2005)

12. Siegal (2003)

2

Why is Attunement So Easy and So Hard?

Attunement is so easy.

Attuning to yourself starts with attending to your immediate sensations, feelings, thoughts, and impulses. Sometimes we are consciously aware of a physical sensation such as a warm ocean current, of an emotion like triumph, of a thought like "I wonder if there is awareness after death?" or of an impulse like wanting some vanilla ice cream. More often we are not consciously aware. If we relax into the moment, we often discover that everything in our field of attention is accompanied by some level of attraction or repulsion, yum or yuck. Neuroscientists call these yums and yucks "prime emotions."[1]

Attuning to self.

What do you sense in your body right now? Are you relaxed, tense, hot, cold, hungry, full, comfortable, or uncomfortable? What emotion are you feeling right now? Are you happy, sad, frightened, irritated, ashamed, joyful, guilty, disgusted, interested, or apathetic? What are you thinking right now? Are you thinking about attunement, about your grocery list, about what you have to do at 10:00, or about why you're feeling what you're feeling? What are your impulses at this moment? Do you want to keep reading, take a nap, eat a snack, call your spouse, or look out the window? If you compassionately accept whatever you're experiencing and organize your attention and behavior right now with the intent to serve what you believe is in the highest good, you are in an attuned moment with yourself.

Attuning to your spouse.

Attuning to your spouse first involves awareness and acceptance of what you are experiencing, and then extending awareness into your spouse and, with caring intent, imagining and accepting what they are sensing, feeling, thinking, and wanting. "Accepting" does not necessarily mean "agreeing" or "complying." You might find what you feel or want repulsive or embarrassing. You might disagree with what your spouse believes, or not be willing to do what they yearn for you to do, and still accept their feelings, thoughts, and impulses. If you feel and accept both your and your spouse's experience and simultaneously organize your thoughts and behaviors to serve what you believe is in the highest good (usually what creates the most love and health for everyone in the moment), you are in an attuned moment with your spouse. Notice how being in an attuned moment with your spouse does not necessarily mean your spouse is in an attuned moment with you. Mutual attunement involves what interpersonal neurobiologists call "resonance," or two or more people being in tune with each other's needs for contact and disengagement.

Mutual attunement.

Mutual attunement tends to happen with caring attention to ourself and another because states of consciousness recruit reciprocal states in others. Caring states tend to evoke caring in another the same way an angry state tends to evoke anger in another. When two people are mutually attuned, they are naturally in sync in the engagement/disengagement dance of life, are reaching for mutual acceptance and understanding, and are literally helping each other's brains integrate and grow.[2]

Attuning to your child.

Attuning to your child is similar to attuning to your spouse. You feel into and accept your own experience, feel into and accept your child's experience, and organize your thoughts and behavior with caring intent. The difference between attuning to children and spouse is that you usually have different responsibilities, authority, and reactions with your child than with your spouse, and your child often has a radically different worldview than either you or your spouse.

Attuned parents are usually guided by the intent of helping their children grow to be happy, healthy, caring, and successful. If this positive intent is accompanied by insight and empathetic connection (what neuroscientist Dan Siegal calls "mindsight"), parents can eventually create attractor states of attunement that soothe and regulate their children's states of consciousness, and tend to influence their children's neural networks to develop complementary states of mutual attunement between parent and child. This literally helps shape children's brains to be healthier and more integrated.[3]

It is the parent's responsibility to consciously reach for empathetic connection and positive intent. Our brains don't fully mature till around age twenty-six. Infants have no conscious awareness. Toddlers have limited, magical, egocentric self-awareness. Elementary school children have increased empathy but limited capacity for self-reflection. Adolescents are still developing in their capacity to "read" others' emotions, and are overwhelmed by the burdens of developing an adult identity.[4] When it comes to holding the responsibility for family attunement, the buck stops with Mom and Dad.

Our masculine and feminine aspects will tend to experience family responsibilities differently.

Our masculine side tends to be motivated to improve attunement skills through feeling a sense of purpose (or mission) to optimally serve self, spouse, and children. In therapy I challenge my more masculine clients to take on this mission because the masculine tends to grow best in the presence of loving challenge.[5]

Our feminine side tends to be motivated to improve attunement skills through yearning for more love in relationships with self, spouse, and children. I honor and cherish this yearning in my more feminine clients because the feminine tends to grow best in the presence of loving praise.[6]

Attunement is so hard.

A friend recently called to ask me to give a talk to a parents' group at a local school. After we took care of business, I asked her about herself and was blown away by what she had recently been through. She and her husband had an eighteen-month-old daughter, and she'd given birth by C-section three months earlier to a son. Weeks after the birth, their son was diagnosed with a kidney abnormality that needed immediate surgery. He came through the operation fine and was currently vigorous and happy. Like most healthy babies, he was growing like a weed and needed to nurse every two hours, leaving no time for uninterrupted sleep. My friend's daughter was more emotionally reactive than her brother and daily would cry for twenty or thirty minutes at a time. She was inconsolable during these episodes, and all her parents could do was keep her physically comfortable and hold her while she screamed. My friend was more tired than she had ever been, more disconnected from her husband than since years before their marriage, and daily was overwhelmed by the needs of her two babies. While all this was happening, their house was being remodeled so that her mother could come stay and help, and workers were constantly in and out of her house, engaging in all the noisy, messy things that contractors do.

If you are a parent, you know what it's like to be chronically sleep deprived, to hold a screaming toddler and feel helpless and frustrated as the crying goes on and on. You feel your relationship with your spouse collapse under the weight of fatigue, frustration, and desperate yearning for time alone and time with each other. In this case there was the further stress of lots of outside intrusions. My friend had previously been both a private and independent person. Now she needed friends, relatives, and health care providers almost constantly just to provide adequate care for her kids and enjoy any kind of life with her husband.

It looks as if there wasn't much attunement going on, right? The remarkable thing about my friend is that, in the midst of all this pain, fear, and chaos, she was staying consistently attuned to herself, her husband, and her children.

Her body was wracked with fatigue, post-surgical pain, and distress over the her children's demands, but she was aware of these things and was doing her best to eat healthy, get rest, and get her personal needs met. She was staying attuned to herself.

Her relationship with her husband had been reduced to tag team parenting and shared child care with snatched moments of sleep. Yet, she felt and accepted his distress over the loss of their old life, and let him know that she understood his pain and yearned to be close in the old ways but just couldn't right now because of all they were going through. She was staying attuned to her husband.

She had a regularly screaming toddler, sleep deprivation, and an infant with a life threatening kidney condition that had required major surgery at three weeks of age. She nursed her baby when he was hungry, held her toddler when she was distressed, and played and sang with them when they wanted to connect. She was staying attuned to her children.

Even though her life felt as if it was careening out of control, she was demonstrating extraordinary skills at attunement to herself, her spouse, and her children. Because of that I am confident that things will just keep getting better for her, her marriage, and her family.

Most people, given these kinds of stressors, will periodically succumb and neglect caring for self, spouse, and demanding babies. Having the conscious intent to serve love and health can bring us back from such collapses and make for integration and increased strength and resilience.

Stress pressures us to enter defensive states of consciousness where we don't feel into ourselves and others and we're not organizing our thoughts and behaviors to be caring. Often attunement is the hardest thing imaginable at just those times when we and the people we love need it the most. Conscious intent to feel into ourselves and others and serve love can always bring us back to caring.

Attunement is relative to our current perspectives and masculine/feminine balance.

Jim and Sally, the couple from Chapter One, stayed in therapy six months and worked hard at harmonizing more effectively to themselves, each other, and Jake. Things got better, and they began to feel that their family was working for all of them. In the twenty-fifth session, when both reported life being "pretty sweet," I suggested that they come in six months later for a check up, but Jim thought that was "unnecessary" and said they'd call when they needed a session.

Three years later Jim called and told me that he and Sally needed to come in for a "tune up." They arrived older, heavier, more relaxed, and more emotionally aware. They maintained eye contact while they talked, and noticed and seemed to care about each other's reactions. After some preliminary catching up (Jake was in kindergarten and their second child, Eric, had been born ten months previously), they began to discuss what had brought them back into therapy:

Jim: "I don't want to sound selfish, but we have no sex life."

Sally: (Speaking with some heat.) "I'm taking care of a five-year-old and a baby. I'm tired all the time. What do you expect?"

Jim: "I know it's hard on you, honey, but I'm putting in fifty hours a week at the office and then trying to help out at home when I can."

Sally: (Softening.) "I know how hard you work, and I appreciate it. This sex thing is just frustrating. What am I supposed to do? Pretend that I'm interested when I'm not? Is that what you want me to be, some kind of hooker?"

Jim: (His face is frustrated and his body is tense, but he's looking right at Sally and trying to solve the problem.) "No, of course not. I want you to be interested. I just don't know what to do. That's why we called Keith."

Keith: "First of all, I want to compliment both of you on how you've grown since we first met. You're mostly aware of your own experience, you're talking right to each other, and you both get that you have an important shared issue that you want to improve. Neither one of you is doing much blaming or distorting. I'm impressed."

Jim: (Obviously both pleased and a little uncomfortable with the compliments.) "Well ... thanks, but, what do we do?"

Sally: "Everybody knows that your sex life suffers when you have kids."

Keith: "That's usually true. How would you like it to be, Sally?"

Sally: (A faint flush appears on her throat and cheeks.) "I'd like time together. I'd like to get enough sleep. I'd like Jim and me to have more of the fun talks we were having before Eric was born. I'd like some romance in my life."

I notice Jim relaxing as Sally talks about what she yearns for. Feminine yearning without anger is usually beautiful to masculine people. I ask him what he's feeling and thinking:

Jim: "It's nice to hear she wants some of the things I want."

First-, second-, third-stage relationships and sexual polarity.

I wasn't kidding when I told them I was impressed. Intimacy, sexuality, family, and children stress us, but they also help us grow. Individuals and couples grow through stages in their ability to love. My favorite teacher in this area, David Deida, says that first-stage relationships are all about "me" and what "I" want; second-stage relationships are all about "we" and what's "fair;" and third-stage relationships are about being our deepest selves and giving our best gifts.[7]

Jim and Sally have grown in the last three years to being more about "we." Jim wants to contribute "his share" to household responsibilities but feels it's "not fair" that he and Sally have no sex life. Sally appreciates Jim's contributions and misses intimacy with him but believes it's "not right" to be sexual with him when she doesn't feel like it. A problem that can arise with egalitarian second-stage relationships is that partners tend to believe the more deeply masculine and more deeply feminine spouses have the same worldviews, responsibilities, and needs. This is usually not the case. To be able to attune successfully to a spouse (or to yourself or a child) it's often necessary to perceive and understand masculine and feminine aspects. This is how I explain it to Jim and Sally:

Keith: "I believe that the purpose of a family is to support the health and growth of all members" (Both Sally and Jim nod.) "Each of us has both masculine and feminine in us, but in our deepest intimacy (like our erotic relationship with our spouse) we are usually either more masculine or more feminine. David Dieda calls this 'our sexual essence.' You, Jim, in your love affair with Sally, have a more masculine essence, while Sally has a more feminine essence. This has huge repercussions on your relationships with everybody, and especially with each other."

Sally: (This offends her sense of second-stage egalitarianism.) "That sounds sexist to me."

Keith: "Really? Would you rather go shopping or watch football? Do you like action movies or relationship movies? Do you want to try new dishes at restaurants or always get what you know you like? Do you choose what to wear because of what's handy or because of how you feel when you're dressing? Do you read romance novels or action novels? Is success or failure more absorbing to you or whether love's happening or not happening?"

Sally: (Laughing.) "OK, I get it. But what does this have to do with our sex life?"

Jim: "And if we're so different, how can we ever solve this problem?"

Keith: "Notice how you want to "solve the problem"? More masculine people crave nothingness, and tend to conceptualize life as a series of problems that need to be solved. A problem is something. Solve it, and you turn it into nothing. Feminine people like relating. A group of women discussing an issue will often avoid obvious solutions so that they can keep processing and relating."[8]

Jim: "That's crazy."

Keith: "No, that's feminine." (Sally nods and smiles at Jim.) "In sexual intimacy, what turns a masculine person on is feminine erotic radiance expressed through pleasure in her body and devotional love towards him. What turns a feminine person on is masculine depth of consciousness expressed through presence, humor, and shadow. Shadow includes those parts of himself that are hard or uncomfortable to perceive. That means he knows and accepts all aspects of himself including his shadow, knows his purpose, knows her, and claims her while making her feel loved and safe. The more thoroughly you inhabit these masculine and feminine poles, the stronger your erotic polarity will be. Because of your histories, your habitual defensive states of consciousness, the stresses and demands of your life, and your lack of knowledge of masculine and feminine practice, your sexual polarity has suffered. To be a good lover, you generally need to be congruent with your pole of erotic polarity in your relationship.[9] Neither of you has either adequate knowledge or sense of personal responsibility to do this."

Sally: "But I like action movies sometimes. I like to order the same things at restaurants a lot."

Jim "Yeah, and I care a lot about whether love is happening."

Keith: "As I said, we all have both masculine and feminine in us, but in our deepest hearts, who are we? Is it more blissful to find meaning at the edge of death or to talk about your friend's relationship with her sister? Are you more attracted to Jim when he can stay connected to you when you're upset but be both caring and unrecoiling, or if he's an open channel of emotion who shows all his feelings through his body." (This image of Jim being Mr. Open channel of emotion is too much for both of them, and Sally groans, "No, I don't think I'd like that.")

Jim: (As a more masculine person, he stays focused on "solving the problem.") "How does all this help us have a sex life?"

Keith: "You remember all the attunement stuff we talked about three years ago?"

Jim: "Sure. We both do it with each other and the kids, and it's wonderful. Feel into your self, feel into the other, focus your thoughts and behavior on what serves the highest good."

Sally: "Except for Jim being so frustrated about sex, it's better than I ever hoped it would be with him and the kids. It's especially useful with Jake, because he gets excited or tired and doesn't know what he needs. I try to tune in and help him. Jim's so much better at it. Jake adores his dad."

Keith: "That's so cool that you do all that. Improving your erotic relationship won't be nearly as hard as what you've already done. All you have to do is go deeper. To attune most deeply to yourself, it helps to know if you are a more masculine or feminine person, and if you are in a more masculine or feminine moment. In erotic polarity, the masculine feels into himself, the moment, and his feminine partner, and offers her direction as to what will create the most love. The feminine partner feels into herself and her masculine partner, and, if he's trustable, shows him her pleasure through her body, and, if he's not, shows him her distress. If the masculine partner feels her distress, he adjusts towards making her feel known and claimed, and safe and loved, until he again feels her pleasure. The better you are at these practices, the more solid your erotic polarity tends to be."

Jim: "This all makes sense." (Sally nods and concurs.) "But no one ever talked about this when I was growing up."

Knowing what our deepest masculine or feminine sexual essence is, and whether we are in a more masculine or feminine moment, helps us enormously in our abilities to attune. In erotic relationships we have responsibilities that are complementary but asymmetrical. To enhance sexual polarity and be a more trustable man, Jim probably needs to take on the responsibilities of being aware and accepting of himself, being present, feeling into Sally, and opening her further when she feels pleasure at his attention (a "yum") or adjusting when she feels distress (a "yuck"). For Sally to enhance their sexual polarity, she probably needs to practice feeling into herself and Jim and, when he's trustable, showing him her pleasure through her smile, tone, posture, breath, and touch, and when he doesn't feel trustable, showing him her distress while staying attuned to him. This way she can discern when he adjusts back to his trustable self and show him her pleasure when he does. Masculine people are nourished and attracted by feminine pleasure, especially when it's directed at them as devotional love. Feminine people are nourished by being pleased, pleasured, or otherwise opened by a trustable, present, masculine person.

Erotic polarity is a big deal. The parental relationship is the center of the family. At the heart of the parental relationship is a love affair that continues (for better or worse) as a core aspect of marriage. In our monogamous society there is usually only one person that is our designated lover. We can have hot polarity or we can allow our love affair to devolve into a depolarized relationship. The parental love affair runs off of each partner's ability to establish and maintain erotic polarity, which, in turn, runs off of how aware each is of their respective deepest sexual essences and how true and responsive they are to those essences.

Who's going to teach this to our children?

Every child has a masculine and a feminine aspect and a deepest sexual essence that is usually more feminine or more masculine. Our deepest essence stays constant while our masculine and feminine aspects ebb and flow throughout the life stages we progress through from birth to death. For instance, second-stage egalitarian men, even though they have a masculine sexual essence, tend to amplify and emphasize their feminine aspect in their intimate relationships, while the converse is true for second-stage women. The skills of identifying, honoring, and inhabiting these elements in healthy ways are difficult, demanding, and tied into many other important developmental lines (such as children's ability to think, care for others, have effective self-reflection, and create mature relationships). How are children going to learn about these central qualities of their personalities and how to interface appropriately and joyfully with other people?

Schools don't teach this. American egalitarian principles essentially forbid education that embraces and explores the profound differences between masculine and feminine. In addition, federal mandates to provide abstinence-based sex education forbid teaching children how to identify and develop their abilities to appropriately inhabit erotic polarity.[10]

Most religious traditions don't teach this. Major religious traditions are uniformly critical (or, at best, ambivalent) about training children in the knowledge and skills they might need to create joyful, erotically fulfilled intimacies with lovers.

Most friends don't teach this. Relying on friends to teach the principles of masculine and feminine practice and erotic polarity is like locking two ten-year-olds in a room and demanding that they spontaneously teach each other calculus.

Most parents don't teach this. Judith Levine in her book *Not For Minors*, reports that 80 per cent of American children have essentially no substantive conversation about sexuality with their parents.[11] If you want to teach these principles and practices to your children, you will be moving into developmental territory that is mostly not supported by our culture. This is often unexpectedly difficult.

We are internally influenced and governed by hundreds of cultural standards that we absorb throughout our lives. Our instinct to inhabit positions on personally important social hierarchies involves internal pressures to conform to the behavioral and moral standards of our chosen social group. Most cultural standards serve love and health. We all understand that it's wrong to lie and steal, and right to help people in need. None of us has to be reminded to wear a shirt to work or not to knock others down on a crowded sidewalk. Some cultural standards cause suffering. For example, it may be admirable to buy a gas-guzzling SUV, acceptable to cheat on taxes, or entertaining to play a cruel practical joke on a classmate.

Most of us were raised with taboos about explicitly discussing sexuality with others and, especially, discussing it with family members. The title of this book, *The Attuned Family: How to Be a Great Parent to Your Children and a Great Lover to Your Spouse*, will be uncomfortable territory for some people because it uses the words "parent" and "lover" in the same sentence. The danger of not moving into such territory is that if, at a given moment, any aspect of a child is ignored or critically judged by either parent, the child is likely to not feel securely attached, creating internal conflict. Put together enough conflicted moments, and children can start internalizing critical judgments of themselves and others that can foster tendencies to block intimacy or be internally and relationally avoidant, ambivalent, or chaotic.

Love can find a way.

If you are attuned to your own masculine/feminine aspects, are aware of and true to your deepest masculine or feminine essence, and can attune with your spouse to support robust and healthy erotic polarity, you are teaching your children how to do the same. Our nervous systems resonate with those of our children and literally teach their brains how to grow. In addition, if we are willing to challenge our own cultural conditioning, we can explicitly include culturally forbidden subjects such as masculine/feminine aspects/essence in attunements within our families as children grow, teaching them age-appropriate lessons about love, polarity, and sexuality at every developmental level. For example, the following family is attuning to sexual issues arising from fourteen-year-old Albert walking into the kitchen to find his parents, Rachel and Harry, in the midst of a passionate kiss. Unlike Jim and Sally who are struggling with young children, Rachel and Harry have two teens and a grade schooler, and, at this point in their family's development, are relatively expert in attunement:

Albert: "Get a room."

Harry: (Initially irritated at being interrupted, senses his son's discomfort with this public display of erotic polarity, feels compassion and attunes to him.) "Sorry Al. Sometimes your mother is just too irresistible." (Rachel smiles and resumes washing the dishes. Albert still looks uncomfortable, so Harry continues.) "What's wrong, son? You seem distressed."

Albert: "I don't know. It just seems weird to see you two scamming on each other."

Rachel: "It's not like you haven't seen it before."

Albert: (He's been taught to feel into himself, and that it's safe to express emotions and thoughts to his parents.) "It feels different now."

Rachel: (She feels interest and concern, perceives Albert's conflicted state, and orients to the parental principles of accepting what is and helping her child grow. This naturally guides her focus.) "What's different?"

Albert: (He has a flash of kissing his girlfriend, Sara, at the party they were at last Saturday night.) "I guess it's 'cause I have a girlfriend."

Harry: (Feeling Albert's need to fit this experience into the story of his life.) "So you know what it's like to really kiss somebody?" (Albert nods awkwardly.) "What bothers you about seeing us do it?"

Albert: "It just seems wrong. I know it's not. But it feels that way."

Harry: "Son, how many of your friends do you think have seen their parents have a serious kiss, gotten uncomfortable about it, and had a frank talk like this?"

Albert: (Surprised by both the question and his answer.) "None of them."

Harry: "We live in a culture that views it as vaguely wrong for kids to see their parents being into each other sexually, and practically forbids conversation about it. We're violating all kinds of cultural taboos today." (Both Albert and Rachel laugh.)

Rachel: (She is a feminine person who naturally focuses on caring, community, and loving connection.) "We try not to be too hot and heavy around you kids, but every once in a while you walk in on us. I'm sorry if we upset you."

Albert: (He's visibly more relaxed. The experience has been adequately processed so that it fits into his personal life story. The injury has been repaired in creating a more complex and compassionate understanding of the moment. He's understanding that he's more sexually mature, and thus more aware of sexual polarity between Mom and Dad. His core values have no problem with this, but his cultural conditioning makes him uncomfortable seeing Mom and Dad erotically connected in this way. They are fine with his discomfort, but want him to understand the complexity of the issue. He feels grateful and relieved.) "It's OK. I guess you have as much right as anyone to scam each other." (They all crack up.)

Harry: "Watch out giving us permission son. Now you have to knock before you walk into the TV room."

Rachel: (Playful, but firm.) "Stop it, Harry. Sometimes you tease too much. Albert, you don't have to knock before you enter any room but our bedroom." (Albert punches his Dad on the arm and they play wrestle for a few seconds, which ends with Albert and Mom tickling Dad until he surrenders.)

Harry: (In mock defeat.) "I give up. I'll stop teasing."

This is how attuned families deal with issues. Feel into yourself and others and focus on what your purpose is in the moment. Albert felt discomfort and knew that his job was to express and resolve what was bothering him. Rachel and Harry were initially turned on in the kitchen (enjoying erotic polarity between Harry's more masculine essence and Rachel's more feminine essence), were embarrassed and a little irritated when intruded upon, and then united in supporting their own experience and helping their son process his discomfort. Through long practice they instinctively acted from the intent to help their son develop. Except for Albert's initial sarcastic comment, there was no blaming, no critical judgments, and no pathologizing of anyone for being sexual or distressed.

Attunement is easy when in a state of healthy response to the present moment and hard when in a defensive state.

One problem I've always had with self-help books, psychotherapy books, and inspirational books, is that they make attunement sound so easy. What am I, some kind of moron that I can't consistently be mindful, compassionate, caring, empathetic, or present? Do I have some kind of personality defect or neurological deficit that leads me into the same fight with my daughter, or into forgetting the same important date with my wife? In all the helping systems I studied over the years the principles are sound, the techniques work when they're practiced, and the authors are positive and supportive. What's so hard about feeling good and doing right?

To add to the confusion, when things work, they seem ridiculously simple. The attuned exchange between Harry, Rachel, and Albert is a good example. What's the big deal? Mindful, caring people had a conversation about parents smooching in the kitchen.

What I've discovered in my life, studies, and tens of thousands of therapy sessions is that when we are in a state of healthy response to the present moment we tend to naturally think and do right according to our current worldview. In states of healthy response to the present moment we learn relatively easily, are more comfortably self-reflective, and relate more naturally.

Our brains are genetically programmed to develop toward freer flow of energy and greater complexity.[12] Complex systems like human brains can move to more efficient organization as their parts are differentiated and then connected.[13] Differentiation is understanding these different parts of ourselves, and integration is accepting and embracing these parts into a larger whole, dedicated to doing right by our emerging standards of what is beautiful, moral, and observably true. In states of healthy response, the integrative processes that support the integration of differentiated parts toward freer energy flow and greater complexity of neural networks are relatively unobstructed. Healthy human development involves regularly experiencing states of internal and interpersonal harmony. It is difficult (sometimes impossible) to reach for harmony when in the grip of defensive states involving amplified or numbed emotions, distorted perspectives and thoughts, and destructive impulses.[14]

Infants rely on parents for emotional and physical regulation. Parents are constitutionally motivated by the sight, sound, and smell of babies to care for them.[15] These amazing processes involve parental states of consciousness teaching children's brains how to organize and grow.

At around fifteen to eighteen months of age, children's brains develop to the point where they can more powerfully block parental connection and feel more emotionally separate from their parents. Some call this the birth of the emotional self.[16] Increasingly after this stage, it requires more conscious cooperation from children to establish mutual attunement, or resonance. This awakening of conscious awareness of emotional separateness can be terrifying and infuriating to toddlers. So begins the long developmental journey toward a secure/autonomous adult self who, ideally, from any state of consciousness, can deliberately feel into self and others with caring intent.

In this sense, the capacity for conscious attunement can be seen as a continuum, with having to rely on others for self-regulation on one end and being able to feel into ourselves and others with caring intent *independent of our own or others' states of consciousness* on the other end. It can also be viewed as a developmental line where the deeper we mature, the more consistently capable we are of attunement in wider ranges of situations and states.

Attuned families have two parents who are relatively skilled at feeling into themselves and others with caring intent, independent of environmental demands or varying states of consciousness. This capacity fits seamlessly into a number of definitions of optimal development and mental health, described variously as "differentiation" by Murray Bowen,[17] "individuation" by Carl Jung,[18] "self-actualization" by Abraham Maslow,[19] and "integration of consciousness" by Dan Siegal.[20]

Problems arise because our brains are so high powered and effective at protecting us.

Ironically, when things get hard, it's often due to the sophistication of our brains and bodies as they've evolved over millennia. Our distant relatives first experienced consciousness in hunter-gatherer groups that lived a harrowing existence on the sparsely forested plains of ancient Africa. Our forebears had to deal with weather, uncertain food sources, predators, other tribes, and each other. Evolutionary psychology and neurobiology have documented how our brains have developed complex, automatic strategies for survival in dangerous environments. How might the following hard-wired human capacities have increased chances for survival (thus enhancing our likelihood of passing on our genes) in hunter-gatherer society?

- Infants tend to stay close and emotionally connected to caregivers.[21]

- Mothers tend to want to hold, caress, and nurture their children.[22]

- When hurt by a sound, touch, feeling, event, or person, our brains react with alarm and the tendency to avoid such pain in the future. When pleased we tend to welcome similar experiences. This process, a part of our implicit memory, begins before birth and happens outside of our awareness *without a sense of something being remembered.*[23] In other words, if a scary dog snarled at me when I was six months old, I might be scared of dogs when I'm twenty-seven and *have no conscious sense of why that is.* If a jasmine-scented caregiver was warm and loving, jasmine might be an especially pleasurable scent for the rest of my life. Many of our automatic attractions and repulsions are governed by implicit learning, where we react without conscious knowledge of anything other than our immediate feelings, thoughts, and impulses while we are actually remembering previous pleasures or distress.

- Human brains, when faced with threat, proceed through three consecutive options: social engagement, fight or flight, and dissociation.[24]

- Men, who through increased strength and aggressiveness were the main hunters in ancestral tribes, think and relate more hierarchically than women.[25] This is an advantage for tribal hunters, since a hunting group needs clearly defined leaders and followers to be able to develop and implement strategy and tactics. Similarly, since hunting requires great dedication to a goal while dealing with many variables, men tend to have a global perspective, while focusing on a single objective. Women (more often communal gatherers, food processors, and caregivers for small children in tribal societies) tend to focus on caring for others, while being more able than men to multi-task, especially with detail oriented, multi-faceted projects.[26]

- Men are drawn to the sight of a female form, hungering to sexually merge with healthy young women. This predisposes them to be attracted to spreading their genes among many women. On the other hand, in the weeks before their mate gives birth, men's prolactin levels (a hormone linked with nurturing) rise 20%, and, in the weeks after birth, their testosterone levels drop a third and their estrogen levels rise, predisposing them to be less aggressive and to bond with and protect their mate and offspring.[27]

- Women are drawn to a trustable masculine presence, someone who seems high status; thus better able to protect her and her children.[28]

- Children mimic expressions, behavior, sound, and touch. We're born with mirror neurons in our brains that influence us to replicate expressions, sounds, movements, and states of mind.[29]

- Starting at age five or six (about the time that the connections between our right and left brain hemispheres mature and our brains undergo their first major pruning of "unnecessary" or "unused" neurons) we begin to value membership in our family enough that we want to adhere to family rules so as to be included in the group. In other words, we grow in the tendency to care whether we are pleasing or distressing others.[30] This crucial step from self-centered to tribe-centered motivates us to cooperate and support the group just as we're getting old enough to be able to make significant contributions to hunting, gathering, infant care, and all the other complex physical, social, and ceremonial demands of tribal life.

- At age eleven or twelve (when adolescence accelerates accompanied by our second round of major neural pruning) we begin to be able to hold opposing concepts simultaneously in our consciousness, start to more assertively question existing rules, and begin to develop our own, more individualistic values and goals. As this happens we are more strongly drawn to inhabit positions in merit based hierarchies.[31] In other words, we are craving to discover and inhabit adult roles in the tribe.

- People are social creatures who require social involvement to grow. The brains of children who do not have adequate physical and emotional contact are literally smaller, less complex, and less responsive than the brains of children with adequate contact.[32]

As you can see, we are programmed to develop in countless, complex ways. We grow through different worldviews, constantly being conditioned by our experience. We are motivated by our natural drives to create meaning, have intimate connections with our family and others, be true to our deepest masculine/feminine essences, and inhabit positions on personally important social hierarchies.

When we are threatened, our brains instinctively react to protect us, using our memory and learning capacities that started at conception and that just keep getting more complex and powerful throughout our lives. Like infants, when threatened we automatically resist change and want others to soothe and care for us. These automatic reactions form the basis of our defensive states that manifest as the amplified or numbed emotions, distorted perspectives and beliefs, and destructive impulses such as the ones we observed with Jim and Sally in their first session.

Defensive states are why it's difficult to stay attuned when we feel threatened. Defensive states are why it's so hard to follow through on all the great suggestions in self-help books. Defensive states interfere with our resolve to love each other wisely and generously all the time.

A simple formula for health and growth: Practice attunement when it's easy; reach for attunement when it's hard.

I encourage my clients to consciously practice attunement with themselves, their spouses, and their children as much as possible. The more we reach for these states, the more we experience them. The more we experience them, the more deeply embedded the neural circuits associated with them become in our brains.[33] The more we inhabit these states, the more we magnetize others to inhabit complementary states. This is important with our children because parental states of consciousness literally teach children's brains how to grow, and important with our spouses because mutual attunement maximizes health, creativity, and love.

Attunement is often effortless in moments of healthy response and can appear impossible in defensive states. We support self-awareness and healthy self-worth when we recognize, honor, and enhance attunement when it's easy and reach for it when it's hard.

1. Siegal (1999)

2. *Ibid*

3. Siegal (2003)

4. Wilber (2000)

5. Deida (1997)

6. *Ibid*

7. Dieda, (1995)

8. Gilligan (1993)

9. Dieda, (1995)

10. Levine (2002)

11. *Ibid*

12. Siegal, (1999)

13. Siegal (2005)

14. Witt, (2005)

15. Lemonick (2004)

16. Wilber, (2000)

17. Bowen, (1961)

18. Jung, (1961)

19. Maslow, (1962)

20. Siegal, (2003)

21. Taylor (2002)

22. *Ibid*

23. Siegal, (1999)

24. Porges (2004)

25. Gilligan, (1993)

26. *Ibid*

27. Brizendine (2006)

28. Deida, (2004)

29. Siegal (2005)

30. Wilber, (2000)

31. Witt, (2005)

32. Siegal, (2003)

33. *Ibid*

3

We Each Live in Our Own Universe

Rachel and Harry's family weren't always able to resolve difficult issues into love and humor. Six years earlier all five family members walked into my office with a lot of problems. That day, Rachel and Harry looked worried and angry. Fifteen-year-old Brian was dressed in baggy gangster clothes and had a palpably contemptuous attitude to the whole therapy process. Eight-year-old Albert sat in the corner and only reacted when four-year-old Hannah teased him enough to drive him out of his apathy. Hannah was active, distracting and interrupted everyone except Brian. When he talked, usually with an angry tone, she kept mostly still:

Keith: "What brings us together." (Brian rolls his eyes, Hannah giggles, and Albert sinks deeper into his chair. Harry looks frustrated, and Rachel looks sad and tired.)

Rachel: "Brian's been smoking pot, drinking, staying out way past curfew with his friends, and his grades have gone down."

Harry: (Education has been his ticket to success. Brian's academic failures scare and frustrate him.) "Gone down is right. He's getting D's and F's when he used to get A's and B's."

Brian: "School sucks."

Rachel: (Looking at Brian, who doesn't meet her eyes, while she talks about him.) "That's been his attitude for the last two years. We've tried everything we know how to do and nothing works. Brian won't work with tutors, he won't finish assignments, and he won't follow our rules."

Keith: "Brian, what's true about all this?"

Brian: "What do you mean?"

Keith: "What's your perspective? Your parents say that you're failing at school, abusing drugs and alcohol, and are out of control at home. What's valid and not valid about what they're saying?" (At this point Hannah starts poking at Albert, who tells her "Stop!" while Hannah keeps poking.)

Harry: "Hannah, stop!" (Hannah temporarily backs away from her brother, but is obviously poised to poke him again.)

Keith: "Harry, I think it would be easier for Hannah to relax and participate if you were sitting with her." (I also think it will be easier for Harry to self-regulate his own distress while he's more connected with his four-year-old daughter. Harry gets up, sits next to Hannah, and puts his arm around her. She fidgets a little and then calms down. I turn back to Brian.) "Well?"

Brian: "Well what?"

Keith: (I feel his hostility and I'm worried. Fifteen-year-olds can get lost in self-destructive states, behavior patterns, and relationships. If they hook up with one of the varieties of oppositional teen tribes that exist in every high school, they can lose their way, wreck their lives, and traumatize their family. In these states of consciousness and life circumstances they often try to avoid their emotional pain by engaging in the most dangerous, uncaring, and self-destructive behaviors imaginable, and not seem aware of the risk or the cost. I repeat my earlier question.) "What's valid about your parents' concerns?"

Brian: "They always exaggerate. They just don't like my friends."

Rachel: "You bet I don't like your friends. They drink and smoke pot with you and do God knows what else. They never come by our house, and, when they do, you're even more rude to me and the family."

Brian: "Fuck you."

Harry: (Not noticing how Rachel, Hannah, and Albert all cringe at his tone, he lashes out at Brian.) "Don't you dare talk to your mother that way!"

Brian: (Apparently relaxed, though I notice sweat beading his forehead.) "Or what?"

Harry: (Hannah starts to cry, and Harry's attention immediately shifts to his daughter sitting next to him. His voice softens.) "It's OK sweetheart. I'm sorry I yelled."

We all grow up in different families.

Each person in this session has a unique worldview and routinely shifts between numerous states of consciousness. These worldviews and states of consciousness share many similar perspectives but are also often wildly different, especially when there is negative arousal involving fear, rage, shame, disgust, boredom, or helplessness.

In exchanges like the one above, it's often hard for a therapist to remember that each family member is capable and experienced in caring. This same family was laughing and joking with each other a week earlier at the movies watching *The Producers.* The night before the session, Rachel came in to kiss Brian good-night and they talked a little and ended with "I love you." Silent Albert was talking enthusiastically and incessantly about baseball to his Dad that very morning. Hannah's teachers describe her as a happy child who cooperates easily in class activities. At this moment in the session, everyone is in a defensive state. There is not much attunement going on. There are a lot of amplified or numbed emotions, distorted perspectives, and destructive impulses. They are five lonely people living in their own worlds. To get a sense of how we develop through stages of thinking, feeling, and relating, let's examine the three children's worldviews, states of consciousness, and abilities to attune, and then listen in to a session where Rachel, Harry, and I talk about how to perceive shifting worldviews.

Two to five; egocentric moving into conformist.

Hannah lives in a world where something is often moral if you can get away with it. She understands the concept of rules and, at four, is increasingly moved to follow them so she can feel accepted in the family system. These are normal, egocentric characteristics of a two-to-six-year-old, growing from wanting everything her way toward also wanting to conform to family standards. Like most little girls, she is moving from being primarily self-centered toward caring for the people in her immediate environment. When she feels distressed (often when other family members are fighting) she has impulses to interrupt and act silly. When Hannah was an infant and Rachel was distracted by the other two children, this kind of behavior often evoked positive attention. Now, years later, the impulse is hard-wired into Hannah's nervous system. Feel distress—act silly. She has practiced it thousands of times, and the neural networks associated with this defense are deeply embedded in her brain. When stressed, she automatically goes to silly/distracting. Neuroscientists call this an "attractor state."[1] Similarly, Hannah feels secure in the arms of her parents. Being held by Rachel or Harry has almost always been a safe haven. This is why she automatically entered a more relaxed state when Harry sat next to her and put his arm around her. This is a positive attractor state, cued by being held by her parents.

Four-year-olds are beginning to understand logic but often lapse into magical or mythical thinking.[2] Hannah believes in the Easter Bunny and gets mad at her parents when the family isn't harmonious because they should be able to fix anything. She has practically no capacity to self-reflect on shifts in her states of consciousness but has learned (mostly through dialog, relating, and storytelling in her family) to often know when she's happy, sad, angry, or ashamed.

Hannah knows girls are different from boys. If asked, she describes concrete differences such as "Boys don't wear dresses. Girls have vaginas and boys have penises. Boys like video war-games and don't like to play tea-party. Girls like to play dress up and Barbies." When confronted with the fact that some girls like war-game videos and some boys like to wear dresses, she gets confused.

Hannah's brain is just reaching the peak of a phenomenal growth period that started at conception. Her right and left hemispheres are more fully connected, her capacity for memory is almost fully developed, and her brain is beginning the first of two major pruning periods when unused (or "excess") neurons will die and be "pruned" from her brain. The next and final pruning period will occur in early adolescence.[3]

Sitting in my office is a mostly secure little girl who doesn't really understand what the session is about. She knows there are fights and strife but, since she has nothing to compare it with, believes that's just the way families are. She hates it when Brian is rude to her parents and internally will blame one or the other for not being fair. She wishes they'd "just be nice to each other." The family adores her and protects her, and she feels morally outraged when someone is mean to her personally. The family rule (not conscious or explicitly stated, but "felt" by all family members) is that Hannah is protected from bad feelings. It required considerable effort on my part to influence Rachel to include Hannah in the session. Rachel wanted to "protect her" from the emotional pain that she (accurately) predicted would be revealed and discussed. I suggested to Rachel that this pain was something that Hannah was experiencing daily at home, that none of the issues would be any surprise to her, and it actually might be soothing and empowering for Hannah if there were some progress that she could observe and participate in.

Hannah can usually feel (but not consciously know) the difference when someone is attuned to her or not, and whether she is in a defensive state or a state of healthy response. Her ability to self-reflect is limited. Her current developmental task in learning attunement is getting progressively more in touch with and naming what she is feeling, thinking, and wanting, and learning the rules of exist-ence from family experience. Children do learn from what parents *say* is right, but how a family lives and relates often has a more profound impact on develop-ment than verbal pronouncements. Of special importance to her development as a feminine person is her ability to stay emotionally connected to another and dis-cern whether the other person is trustable or not. The ability to sense this in a masculine person, and offer trust and warmth in response will be central to her capacity to establish and maintain healthy erotic polarity as an adolescent and adult.

Harry and Rachel can support Hannah's development by giving her honest feedback, reflecting her own emotional states back to her (for instance, "You seem happy, sad, angry, or grateful right now"), telling her stories about her feel-ings, thoughts, and behaviors, and consistently attuning to her with the intent of supporting her development as a happy, successful, caring person.

Six to eleven; conformist moving toward rational.

Albert lives in a world that's usually pleasant, but regularly confusing and unfair. Brian sometimes pushes him around, and his parents are often ineffectual in pro-tecting him. Harry tells Rachel to "let the boys work it out on their own," not realizing that this means allowing Brian to dominate Albert. As a result, Albert has developed a defensive attractor state of invisibility. As he demonstrates in the therapy session, he reflexively becomes passive and unobtrusive when there are dangerous painful emotional currents flowing in his family. When Albert is not threatened or stressed, he has the attractor state of happy engagement, and loves to talk about his passions for baseball and dinosaurs.

Elementary school age children care deeply about fairness and following the rules, and are quite strict in their beliefs about enforcement.[4] Albert is outraged that Brian doesn't get punished when he says and does things that would get Albert major consequences, or when Hannah "gets away with stuff" just because she's young and adorable.

This strict interpretation of rules reflects the concrete, black and white way Albert thinks. He doesn't reflect much about inner life, complex conflicting char-acteristics of individuals, or different perspectives of the same event. While believing in following the rules, he rarely questions the legitimacy of rules unless they are blatantly unfair. Such questioning will likely accelerate through adoles-cence as he develops the ability to hold opposing perspectives simultaneously in his consciousness. Now he is concrete.[5] When asked to describe his friend, Dominic, he says, "Dominic is eight and lives three houses down. He has a little brother and two dogs. We play baseball almost every day. I like him; he's my best friend."

Albert assumes that his parents love him, but also that they "favor" Brian because "They let Brian get away with anything." He knows everyone in his family loves one another, and, when his friend Dominic called Brian an "poophead" (a term Albert had himself used for Brian the previous week), Albert defended his brother without self-reflecting on any paradox.

Albert, like Hannah, assumes boys and girls are profoundly different. Boy's "acting like girls" is "gay" and shameful. Boys being tough, strong, and unrecoiling is admirable. Where Hannah is growing from egocentric to caring for others, Albert has matured from egocentric to believing he, his family, and his friends have rights that should be honored.[6] When the girls in his class argue while playing, they often stop the game. When Albert and the boys argue during a game (he feels secure enough in his own age cohort to stand up for himself and be visible) they debate like little lawyers until "rights" are determined, and then they continue to play.

Sexual talk and references are considered "gross" by Albert and his friends around adults, while secretly with each other they find them fascinating and interesting. Albert is quite proud that he can pee farther than his three best friends, but unconsciously assumes that sharing such information with his parents is forbidden. He has had sexual dreams and occasional fantasies, but feels automatic shame and embarrassment and does not even share this material with friends.

Albert's brain is growing in size and complexity as he approaches his second major round of neural pruning that will occur between ten and twelve. He uses logic regularly, is contemptuous of magical thinking (like believing in the Easter Bunny), but has no problem with the concept of a God that personally answers prayers. He is not consciously aware of his "becoming invisible" attractor state when it happens, and will be surprised and confused when I point it out to him later in the session.

An attuned family is organized with the kids having age-appropriate rights and responsibilities that are supervised and enforced by fair but firm parents who also support each other's development. Albert instinctively feels how Brian's out-of-control behavior can dominate the family and create an unhealthy hierarchy with Brian in charge. This leaves Albert less respectful of his parents, less secure in his family, and less clear about what his rights and responsibilities should be or really are at any given moment.

Include and transcend.

Development proceeds in an "include and transcend" fashion. Our brains are too efficient, and our learning is too effective for us to throw out any worldview, skill, habit, or defense. This makes good evolutionary sense, since there is validity in all worldviews, use for all behaviors, and situations were all defenses are optimal. Albert will never lose any capacity or tendency that he has learned or developed. Instead, he will envelop current capacities in new, larger, selves that will each include the "old" Albert as a vital part of an emerging whole. This is how it is on most developmental lines such as our moral line of development or our cognitive line of development.[7] Morally, we never lose our capacity to be selfish; we include our capacity to be selfish in a larger self that usually finds caring more beautiful and good than selfishness. Cognitively, we never lose our capacity to think magically; we include our capacity to think magically in a larger self that usually finds rational thought more true than magical thought. Such include-and-transcend rhythms can be seen on all other lines of development (some estimate there are over twenty interconnected developmental lines) such as our psychosocial line[8], our needs line, our values line, and our spiritual line.[9]

Albert's developmental work in learning attunement includes and transcends what Hannah is learning. He is still learning to develop awareness of his own feelings, thoughts, and impulses. At eight, this capacity is in the process of being included in the larger ability to feel his own experience while experiencing empathy for others. Albert is learning to better sense into what another person might feel, think, and want. He can understand the concept of organizing his intent to serve the highest good but can rarely remember that agenda when in defensive states.

Harry and Rachel can support Albert's emerging abilities by attuning to themselves, each other, and Albert, by healing the wounded hierarchies in their family (not letting distressed children call the shots, and by firmly setting and enforcing fair rules), and by discussing with him what he and others are feeling, thinking, and wanting. Such self-reflective dialog has been shown to create more self-aware children and more bilateral connections between the right and left hemispheres in children's brains.[10]

Eleven to seventeen; rational moving toward pluralistic.

Brian has not gone easily into adolescence. He loved being a boy who played sports, enjoyed being the biggest, oldest child in his family, and looked forward to family camping trips to the mountains and beach. As teenhood swept him up like a wave, a number of things happened to dramatically unbalance his life.

The neural pruning and increased cognitive capacity of eleven to thirteen confronted his black and white elementary school thinking with bewildering shades of gray. Being able to hold competing concepts simultaneously in his consciousness led to him doubting many treasured beliefs. His parents weren't as strong and right as he assumed. His family didn't seem as fun as it used to. The world seemed to be a corrupt place. It was easy and fashionable with friends to be cynical about middle school, high school, and the world in general.

These reactions, if examined self-reflectively with compassionate adults, lead adolescents into reevaluating principles and beliefs and creating new, more complex and individualistic systems and identities. If unobstructed by mood disorders or defensive patterns, these new systems tend to be egalitarian, multicultural, and idealistic; in other words, the best aspects of college students and older teens.

If contaminated with unacknowledged emotional pain and distorted perspectives, avoided through denial and/or suppression, or done mostly with other distressed teens, this reevaluation can lead to cynicism and self-destructive thoughts and behaviors.

Brian had always had some capacity for anxiety and depression but, as an elementary school student, it was manageable. He naturally had lots of mood balancing activities built into his life. He was physically active every day, which reduces anxiety and depression and builds self-esteem.[11] He was a high-status member of his family (the oldest child) and of the group of children he played with in his neighborhood (his house was a meeting place, his backyard was a playground, and he was a leader in many activities). Feeling high status reduces anxiety and depression and builds self-esteem. Brian could talk to his parents about most topics, and emotional language and self-reflection were a part of family life. Open, self-reflective talk about emotionally charged issues reduces anxiety and depression, and supports maturation in how we think and relate.[12] Becoming a better soccer player and tennis player were important goals for him, giving him a sense of purpose. As a more masculine person, having a sense of purpose and feeling progress were soothing for him.[13]

All of this changed with adolescence. Since we feel our emotions more strongly as puberty advances, Brian's anxiety and depression began to become more intense at eleven and were no longer adequately regulated by the above activities. Also, Brian had the common adolescent experience of having his biological clock reset forward, so that he naturally wanted to go to sleep later and wake later. Since it was impossible to rise later due to school schedules, Brian began to accumulate sleep debt, which aggravated his anxiety and depression, thus creating more problems in going to sleep.[14] Anxiety about whether he would go to sleep or get enough sleep led to further sleep difficulties and more anxiety and depression. Added to this was the fact that Brian was feeling intense sexual urgency. He was masturbating daily, feeling shame and confusion about his sexual activities and fantasies, and, since explicit talk about sex was tacitly forbidden in his family, had no one to process this with.

At thirteen, Brian's best friend, Shaun, got some pot from his older brother (about a third of drug users first try drugs with a family member) and shared it with Brian. Marijuana is a hypnotic drug that (among other things) increases the amount of dopamine in brains. Dopamine is a neurotransmitter that enhances pleasure, and while intoxicated, Brian felt dramatically less emotional pain than when sober. Further since pot, like all drugs, is a feminizing substance in that it pulls a person into their body and immediate sensory gratification, it partially answered Brian's intense feelings of sexual urgency and craving for feminine contact. He began to smoke every chance he had and hid it from his parents. He and his friends started to routinely steal alcohol from their parents, and began to experiment with combining the substances. It was so inconceivable to Rachel and Harry that their little boy would be using drugs and alcohol, that it was months before they suspected he was involved. By then Brian had a peer group of likeminded adolescents who hid much more than their substance use from adult society. Once a capacity for hiding from parents is established and supported by a peer group, kids tend to hide lots of difficult or emotionally charged material from adults. Brian's grades plummeted, he dropped out of tennis and soccer, and he stopped going to his parents with distressing emotional issues.

Even though marijuana temporarily creates euphoria, I've observed that daily use actually worsens anxiety and depression, resulting in more craving for the temporary relief of smoking pot. Brian's temperamental capacity for emotional pain, plus the emotional amplification and sleep problems of adolescence, plus the disenchantment of losing treasured childhood beliefs, activities, and meaning, plus the loss of regular exercise and balanced diet as mood regulators, plus the loss of his parents as emotional support sources, plus sexual urgency, shame, and conflict, plus addiction to pot and alcohol abuse, plus a cynical peer group that was hostile to adult society, created a perfect storm of adolescent pain that manifested in the family as Brian turning from Dr. Jekyl into Mr. Hyde.

Like many children and adolescents, Brian's pain was expressed through problems at school and home. By blocking himself emotionally from his parents he lost the benefit of their attunements and began to evoke progressively more of their defensive states of anger and blame. For two years Rachel and Harry tried what had been effective in the past; processing, lectures, boundaries, and coordination with school and sports. To their horror, nothing worked, and Brian just kept getting more angry, depressed, and out of control. This finally landed them in my office.

Since Brian's current level of self-reflection involved barricading himself in the cynical, hostile narratives of his peer group (resulting in an attractor state of closed off, combative hostility when challenged by his parents) he had effectively blocked himself from many of the benefits of parental attunement. The following is an exchange we had in an individual session after their initial family meeting:

Keith: "You seem unhappy."

Brian: "What do you care?"

Keith: "Are you angry at me at this moment?"

Brian: "I don't want to be here."

Keith: "I disagree. You've been practically demanding something like this for years."

Brian: (This piques his interest.) "What are you talking about?"

Keith: (I'm aware of my concern for him, and fear of his danger to himself. Feeling into him, I sense a well of loneliness and hurt beneath a layer of anger. I want to open him to clearer, more honest perspectives. In the face of my attunement, he relaxes a tiny bit.) "I know you're pissed at your parents, but you have to admit that they love you, right?" (Brian nods reluctantly.) "From what I understand, you went from being a happy, successful kid into being a hostile, oppositional, dishonest, chronically unhappy teenager who's failing at school, appears to be drinking and addicted to pot, and who is willing to take dangerous risks with your friends who have essentially no adult supervision. What would you do if your son did what you're doing?"

Brian: (Typically of many kids who are programmed to resist authority, he literally doesn't hear my question.) "I just want them to leave me alone and let me live my life."

Keith: (I relax as we begin a dialog. At least I've engaged him in a conversation.) "Maybe you could describe to me the life you want."

Brian: "I want them to leave me alone and let me do what I want with my friends."

Keith: "How about school?"

Brian: "School's such bullshit. Nothing I learn there is worth anything."

Keith: "So you'd like to drop out?"

Brian: "I could take the exit exam and get a job."

Keith: "Doing what?"

Brian: "I don't know, something."

Keith: "Like what?"

Brian: "Something."

Keith: "If you were a father and your son's career plan was to drop out of high school at fifteen, get whatever job a dropout can get, smoke pot daily, and hang out with his friends who seem to have similar ambitions, what would you do?"

Brian: (Again he doesn't register the question.) "I just want them to leave me alone."

Keith: (I feel relatively well connected at this point, so I decide to press against his defense.) "Do you realize that you didn't hear my question both times I asked it?"

Brian: (He looks a little surprised.) "What question?"

Keith: "I asked what you would do if you were a parent with a son like you."

Brian: (He hears me this time, but falls into his familiar narrative.) "I'd let him do what he wants. It's my life. I should be able to do what I want."

Keith: "You, like most masculine people, want freedom. I'm with you on that; I'm a masculine person and freedom's important to me. You're wrong about what you'd do if you had a son like you."

Brian: "How do you know?"

Keith: "Your parents are good at loving babies and little kids. You were well loved as you grew. When someone has been well loved as a child, they usually grow up to responsibly love their children. If you had a son heading into depression, failure, and self-destruction, you'd try to stop him and help him be happy and successful."

Brian: (He can't deny the truth of this, so, under the stress of a new perspective, he naturally moves into his defensive attractor state of hostile challenge.) "There's nothing they can do. It's my life. They want me to take antidepressants. They complain about me smoking ganja, and they want me to take drugs!"

Keith: (Brian has solid values programmed into his nervous system. Judging from his past behavior he has the ability to be successful in most ways. He's clearly depressed, which distorts perspectives and resists positive change. I want to gauge the possibility that he can cooperate with me and his parents to improve his life, so I challenge his masculine core.) "You're underestimating both their power and their love for you. Parents will do what it takes to save their children."

Brian: (This sounds like a threat. He's been hearing empty threats for two years and feels cynical disregard of anyone's ability to force him to do anything.) "What can they do? Lecture me? Ground me? Take away my allowance?" (He laughs and I join him. Taking away his allowance is a ludicrous image.)

Keith: "If you can't get a hold of your life, they're capable of shipping you off to a special school where you will be forced to be healthy, self-reflective, successful, and caring. Such a place would also probably insist you take antidepressants. Sometimes meds work like magic. In my opinion, you are suffering from depression, and are self-medicating to a certain extent with pot which, by the way, just makes depression worse."

Brian: (He looks a little alarmed, but still blusters.) "They wouldn't dare."

Keith: (I'm feeling connected and more positive because Brian and I are now having a frank discussion about him.) "Brian, I've had this conversation before with a number of teenagers. Parents do what it takes to save their children. These schools cost three to five thousand dollars a month, take kids for eighteen months to three years, and are all over the place. I guarantee if you don't begin working with people you trust to be happier, healthier, and more successful, you'll be entering a place like that within the next six months."

Brian: (Now thoroughly alarmed.) "Why are you saying all this? Did my Dad tell you to threaten me?"

Keith: "Not at all. I'm trying to save you a lot of struggle and hassle, and save your parents a hundred thousand dollars and the loss of their son for two years."

Brian: (This overloads his system. When our emotional window of tolerance is exceeded, we often collapse into shame, humiliation, and rage expressed through our defensive states.) "There's no way they're going to do that."

Never underestimate parental love.

Four months later Brian was being escorted by a professional escort service to Mountain View School in Utah. He stayed there for a year and a half before he finally came home. During that time he remained abstinent from drugs and alcohol and engaged in a program that forcibly removed him from his destructive peer group and immersed him in an alternative culture. This new culture demanded honest self-reflection, success, and acceptance of everyone's right to be respected, within a rigid hierarchy based on the teachers' evaluation of authenticity, honesty, healthy self-understanding, and caring for others.

While he was gone, I worked with his family on opening up closed areas and healing from the traumas of the past two years. One aspect of the work was teaching Harry and Rachel that everyone in their family had different worldviews at different times, and that it was their job as parents to cultivate awareness of everyone's unique perspectives. I was frank about my belief that they had responsibilities to attune and respond to themselves, each other, and each child. Like many couples, the greatest difficulties Harry and Rachel encountered were in attuning to each other. Here are Harry and Rachel in their third session after Brian was taken away to Mountain View:

Harry: "Now Albert's acting up."

Keith: "What do you mean?"

Harry: "He's acting snotty sometimes, and not minding when we tell him to dump the trash or put his dishes away."

Rachel: "It's not that bad, but he's has been acting different. I asked him if anything was wrong, and he said he missed Brian. It's strange, when Brian was here, Albert complained about him all the time."

Keith: "It makes sense to me. Albert's in the five to eleven conformist period where he's a conservative." (Since both Harry and Rachel tend to be pluralistic politically, which means they are multi-cultural, non-hierarchical, consensus seeking, and unconsciously intolerant of opinions other than their own, they find this funny.) "He doesn't like change, and probably is unconsciously stepping into the role that Brian has had the last three years."

Harry: "What role is that?"

Keith: "The role of the problem child."

Rachel: "Oh no. Not another one. I couldn't live through the last three years again."

Harry: "I guess we need to get on him more."

Keith: "I disagree. I think you need to attune better. He's having amplified feelings, distorted perspectives, and destructive impulses. Instead of examining them, you probably find them so alarming that you're pushing them away. I suggest when he's going to sleep, or when you're driving in the car, to ask him how the family's different and how he's different with Brian gone."

Harry: "I'm not going to let him get away with being snotty and disobedient."

Keith: "Harry, one of your blocks to attunement is that, when the kids break rules or act disrespectfully, you use a contemptuous tone when you deal with them."

Harry: "No I don't." (Rachel starts to laugh, and Harry looks genuinely puzzled.) "What?"

Rachel: "You do use a contemptuous tone." (She gets more serious.) "I don't like it."

Harry: "The kids need a strong father."

Keith: "They have a strong father. You need to exercise that masculine firmness with compassion, rather than contempt. Do you know when you're using that tone?"

Harry: "No, but I can tell when everyone (he glances at his wife) including Rachel, tunes me out." (Rachel looks as if she's been caught doing something wrong.)

Keith: "You guys don't realize that you're wasting a resource here. Harry, I know you are listened to more respectfully when you use a compassionate

tone. I believe you when you say that you're unaware of talking contemptuously. Rachel, you're probably almost always right when you think Harry's
using an ineffectual tone. You both could use this knowledge to be stronger
and more effective with the kids. Also, as an added bonus, it would improve
your sex life."

Harry: "Whoa, you just lost me. How does me using a compassionate tone
with the kids help our sex life?" (Rachel and I smile briefly at each other. She
knows that he's more attractive to her when he's caring, and less so when he's
critical.)

Keith: "Ask Rachel." (Harry looks at her expectantly.)

Rachel: "I feel closer to you when you're kind with the kids." (Harry looks
interested.)

Keith: "Rachel, if you were brave enough to show Harry when he's pleasing
you or turning you off, and, Harry, if you were wise enough to adjust
towards compassion when Rachel was turned off, everybody would do better. In all our sessions, Albert's almost always responded positively to compassion. Kids have a sense of personal dignity that they need to have
respected."

Harry: (Looking into Rachel's eyes.) "If you tell me, I'll try." (She nods
uncertainly.)

Keith: "It's better if you just show him. Try it now. Show him your 'pleased'
expression." (Rachel smiles and lights up like a Christmas tree. Harry and I
share an appreciative glance.) "Now, show him you're 'yuck, I don't like
that' expression." (Rachel's face freezes.)

Harry: (He's surprised.) "That's your 'yuck' expression?" (Rachel nods.) "Oh
oh. I've seen that way too much. I never really knew." (He's getting a new
glimpse of Rachel's worldview, with the possibility of endless new surprises if
he can remember to read her expressions non-defensively.)

Keith: "The thing is, you can't argue with her that your don't mean to be
offensive. That hurts her even more. You need to make it safe for her to
show you her 'yuck.' You do that by figuring out what's valid about her reaction and adjusting toward compassion right now. If you do, you'll soon feel
her 'yum' unless she's so hurt that she's stopped attuning to herself or you."

Harry: "But I don't mean to be offensive."

Keith: "We all live in different universes, and none of us is ever completely aware of all the messages we put out; especially non-verbally. In presentations, fifty-five percent of the message is entirely non-verbal.[15] It's probably more like seventy percent in marriages. If we're lucky, we have an intimate person who'll show us if we're opening or closing the moment. If they're lucky, when they show us, we'll be deep enough to not attack or defend, but shift towards presence and compassion."

Harry: "Sometimes it's hard being patient with the kids."

Keith: "You and Rachel are both self-aware adults, and look how hard it is to understand each other's worldview sometimes; especially when you're in defensive states. Your kids are all in different developmental stages morally, cognitively, interpersonally, and kinesthetically, just to name a few developmental lines. Added to that, they all regress to younger, more conflicted perspectives when they're in defensive states. When Albert is scrunched down and quiet, he's in his 'invisible' defense, and you know how hard it is to get him to talk." (Both nod.) "Impatience, contempt, and criticism make that worse. Compassion, even if you have to set a boundary, or insist that he have a consequence, opens him up."

Rachel: "I've noticed that with him."

Keith: (Playfully.) "So, Harry, the key is that when notice you're losing it and adjust toward compassion, or notice Rachel's 'yuck' and adjust, you're improving your sex life." (Both laugh.)

This is what happens when attunement is the organizing principle of family relating. Parents naturally begin to understand and support different worldviews, states of consciousness, and masculine/feminine polarity. Feeling into ourselves with acceptance, and then feeling into each other with positive intent will lead us where love needs to go.

1. Siegal (1999)

2. Wilber (2000)

3. Siegal (1999)

4. Wilber (2000)

5. *Ibid*

6. *Ibid*

7. Wilber (2000)

8. Erikson (2000)

9. Wilber (2000)

10. Siegal (2003)

11. Tourneau (2001)

12. Cozolino (2002)

13. Deida (1997)

14. Dement (1999)

15. Gelb (1988)

4

Brains are Social Organs

Our brains are always relating. We relate individually with ourselves, interactively with our environments, and interpersonally with others.

We relate with ourselves.

Individually, we learn, grow, and live in relation to numerous aspects of ourselves. We naturally move from one state to another, one thought to another, one memory to another, and one anticipatory fantasy (literally, "remembering" the future[1]) to another. Each state, thought, memory, or anticipation evokes (or recruits) a variety of reactions in our brains and bodies. I'm relaxed and reminded of sitting on my couch in the sunlight, which evokes warm satisfied feelings and the thought that there isn't time today to sit in the sun, which evokes frustration, which reminds me of how I couldn't get my computer to format the way I wanted and I'd better start trying to fix that now, which evokes anticipatory anxiety and the "remembering the future" vision of me sitting helpless at the keyboard in an hour, and so on. In these examples, various aspects of myself are interrelating in the past, present, and future.

We relate with our environments.

We relate interactively with our environments in every state except deep dreamless sleep, where we are aware of no objects. A cold wind blows and I think of getting my coat, which leads me to the closet and finding my coat fallen on the floor, which evokes irritation and concern I might have ripped my coat, which causes me to check it out to see if it's intact, and so on. In these examples, I enter different states of consciousness relating to various aspects of my environment.

We relate with others.

We relate to others in countless ways, mostly nonverbal. I look at you, feel affection, and smile. Mirror neurons in your brain mimic my state of mind, which causes your brain to enter a complementary state of being pleased to see me.[2] I look distracted and you feel faint anxiety which cues a thought that I might be mad at you, which is reflected in your distressed expression, which evokes a sense of defensive irritation in me and the thought that you might be "unfairly" mad at me, and so on. These examples reflect fluid shifts of complementary states that our brains flow in and out of in relation to each other.

Conscious intent helps direct development.

Where our brain takes us in relation to ourselves, our environments, and others is influenced by previous learning (neural networks that we've experienced, "practiced" by repetition, and consolidated into permanent memory), and our natural impulses to survive, relate, create meaning, and be true to our deepest selves. Often, how we relate is profoundly influenced by our conscious intent.

As you can see in all the interpersonal situations we've explored so far, psychological states literally attract and recruit complementary states. If you don't find this scary, try looking at your most outraged, critical expression in the mirror, and then attend to how it affects your feelings, thoughts, and impulses. If you don't find this inspiring, try looking at your most tender expression in the mirror, and then attend to your reactions.

Every time we inhabit a state of consciousness, we are "practicing" that state of consciousness and deepening the neural networks associated with it.[3] Each state we inhabit can evoke complementary states in others. Why is it that optimism, gratitude, and caring for others are the qualities most associated with happy people?[4] These states of consciousness are self-reinforcing, pleasurable experiences which tend to evoke positive responses and associations from ourselves and positive associations with our environments. They predispose us to feel and evoke pleasurable connections with others, which tend to evoke deeper feelings of optimism, gratitude, and caring in us, and so on. Psychologist Daniel Pink, in his research on luck, has found that lucky people tend to practice mindfulness, listen to inner experience and intuition, expect good things to happen, believe they can create some positive outcome from misfortune, and are open to possibilities around them.[5] Imagine yourself in the presence of a mindful, intuitive, optimistic, creative person. What complementary states might such a person evoke in you? I imagine myself more likely to enjoy and trust him or her, thus predisposing me support them; in other words, to help them be more lucky.

Mindsight, mindfulness, and attunement.

Daniel Siegal, in his book *The Developing Mind,* defines "mindsight" as insight and empathy.[6] Jon Kabat-Zinn defines "mindfulness" as "Being aware in the present moment, with purpose, and without judgment."[7] Not surprisingly, these abilities seem to involve the same middle prefrontal cortex area of the brain.[8] Mindsight is, to some extent, a necessary aspect of attunement. Attunement requires the combination of self-reflection and empathy toward others and self (compassionate understanding of different aspects of self can be considered "self-empathy"). A crucial added component of attunement is *conscious intent.*

An attuned moment with myself is one where I have awareness and acceptance of self (I am both self-reflective and empathetic to my own inner aspects), plus the *intent* to organize my thinking and doing to serve the highest good. An attuned moment with you is one where I have awareness and acceptance of myself, am feeling into you with the goal of knowing and accepting what you feel, think, and want, plus the *intent* of organizing my thinking and behavior to do right. A mutually attuned moment is when we are both engaging in this simultaneously.

States recruit complementary states.

As meaning-making creatures, we automatically organize our thinking, remembering, and behaving to be consistent with whatever state we're in. If I'm angry with you for criticizing my dog for his shrill yipping, I am naturally going to organize my thinking and remembering to support my anger (you didn't send me a birthday card this year, and you ignored my new outfit the last time we met, which means you are uncaring and probably don't like me). As I organize my thinking and remembering to support my anger, I will naturally have impulses that are consistent with my experience (I don't want to give you a birthday card, and I don't want to attend your party next Saturday). If I approach you with anger and critical judgment, I will probably recruit a complementary defensive state on your part of wanting to defend yourself, attack me, or get away from me.

If my *conscious intent* is to serve the highest good, I will still feel irritated at you for criticizing my dog, but I'm likely to organize my thinking and doing differently, which will have profound impacts on both of our states of consciousness. I might challenge myself to have compassionate understanding of me and you. This supports self-reflection on how I have a tendency to take some things too personally. This leads to changing my angry narrative to the belief that the most likely explanation of the distressing events is that you're understandably irritated by my dog's shrill yipping (I don't like it myself), you've been so busy that you probably just forgot my birthday, and anyone could have not noticed that I had on a new outfit. I might resolve to have a self-reflective talk with you so I can feel affectionate connection with you again. As I reach for compassionate understanding, and direct my intent towards what serves everybody, I start to feel less angry and more understanding of how each life has its own demands. I begin to feel more relaxed and caring, and to have impulses to engage in more constructive and less destructive behaviors. If I approach you in this state, I'm likely to recruit a complementary state in you.

Since every time we enter a state of consciousness we are practicing that state, deepening the neural networks involved with that state, and recruiting complementary emotions, thoughts and impulses in ourselves and others that further support this state, what states we inhabit have staggering consequences on our relative happiness, clarity of perception, relational satisfaction, and developmental progress. Indeed, research associates mindfulness with decreased stress, increased immune function, better cardiovascular health, and better relationships.[9]

Attunement maximizes states of healthy response to the present moment and minimizes defensive states.

The following exchanges happen on a Sunday afternoon at Rachel and Harry's house, four months after Brian left for Utah. Hannah is having a playdate with her friend Emily, and Albert and his friends Sam and Aaron are playing pitch and run in the back yard. Harry's out playing his weekly game of golf, and Rachel is at the kitchen table finishing up the family taxes (she has a degree in accounting, works twenty hours a week as a bookkeeper, and handles the bulk of the family finances):

> Hannah: (Walking into the kitchen, her face is scrunched up in distress, recruiting complementary reactions in Rachel of irritation and concerned responsibility. It's usually irritating to be interrupted in the midst of a task, but she cares for Hannah, wants her to have good times with her friends, and feels responsible to organize and monitor those times). "Mommy, Emily won't play with me."

> Rachel: (She feels her own experience, feels into Hannah's yearning to have fun play with Emily and her distress that "Emily won't play", and decides she should "Help the girls work it out." She turns in her chair, takes a deep breath, and gives Hannah her full attention.) "Why won't she?"

Hannah: (Relaxing immediately in the presence of Rachel's attunement, she enters a more collaborative and less distressed state.) "I want the Bridal Barbie and she has it, and won't give it to me."

Rachel: (*I hate Barbies. Come on, Rachel, the girls love them; help them work it out.*) "That must be frustrating, even though it is her Barbie. Let's go talk to her about it." (Mother and daughter walk hand in hand into the family room which is strewn with dolls, two playhouses, and some dress up clothes. Emily is holding a Ken doll in one hand and Bridal Barbie in the other.) "Hi Emily, looks like Ken and Barbie are getting married."

Emily: "No, they're having a party, see." (Rachel admires the tableau of a rock and roll band next to the dance area where two other Barbies and a Curious George are displayed. Hannah's egocentric irritated state is restimulated by the sight of Bridal Barbie, and she tugs at her mother.)

Hannah: "I want Bridal Barbie."

Emily: (The angry demand recruits a complementary egocentric defensive state in Emily.) "She's my Barbie!" (Hannah tears up.)

Rachel: (She's frustrated because she knows that patience is required and she wants to get back to the taxes. On the other hand, she's clear in her intent. Right now, supporting the girls having a good time and helping them learn from the situation is the right thing for her to do. Four-to-six-year-olds are moving from egocentric to conformist developmentally, and so they are learning to establish fairness under the rules, but often need a powerful figure, like a parent, to resolve conflict and provide guidance.) "Let's talk about what to do. Bridal Barbie does belong to Emily, and it's up to her to decide what to do with her, but I know that you want that Barbie right now, Hannah, and it's frustrating for you to not be able to play with her." (Hannah nods. Both girls are relaxing in the presence of a non-critical, compassionate, attuned parent. This recruits more caring states in both of them. Rachel offers a possible solution.) "Maybe you could share?"

Emily: (Feeling magnanimous in this more caring state, she holds out the Barbie to Hannah.) "You take her. I can use Cowgirl Barbie." (She picks up the other doll. Hannah happily grabs Bridal Barbie.)

Rachel: "That's very generous of you Emily." (Emily smiles shyly in response to the praise.) "What do you say, Hannah?"

Hannah: (Staring at the doll, she whispers.) "Thank you."

Rachel: (She feels a tingle of irritation which, in her attuned state, suggesting to her that something more needs to be done here. The apology doesn't feel right.) "Hannah, I think it's better to look at Emily, think about how she's sharing, and say 'thank you' like you really mean it." (Hannah, who's feeling quite mellow with Bridal Barbie in her hand, looks at her friend, smiles dazzlingly, and gives her a heartfelt tone.) "Thank-you, Emily." (Emily smiles in return, and Rachel goes back to the taxes.)

How Rachel handled her irritation at being interrupted reveals a central aspect of attunement. We never lose our defensive capacities, but we can grow so that we can recognize egocentric or defensive reactions, and accept them while not identifying with them. Instead, we identify with our larger self that wants the highest good for everyone. This disidentification with immature, destructive aspects of self (while still compassionately accepting them in our "community of selves") and identification with a mature, caring self reflects movement towards a more integrated brain. Individual brains naturally tend to integrate towards freer flow of energy and more complex systems, unless we indulge defensive states.

Attunement is a moment-to-moment, lifelong process. No one ever completely masters it, and all of us are regularly challenged to improve. Just as Rachel settles into the taxes, a baseball shatters the kitchen window, spreading glass all over the kitchen table, and freaking Rachel out:

Rachel: (Frightened and angry, she yells out the window.) "God damn it Albert, get in here!" (Several boy voices are talking simultaneously in the back yard, and Albert slowly opens the kitchen door with Sam and Aaron standing well back.)

Albert: "I'm sorry, Mom, Sam was trying to steal third, and I overthrew Aaron." (Sam in the background to Aaron: "That means I'm safe.")

Rachel: (Still angry and scared, she attacks him.) "How many times have I told you to not throw towards the house? What do I have to do, tattoo it on your forehead?" (Sam and Aaron think this is funny and start to giggle. This exceeds Albert's window of tolerance for public chastisement, and he goes into his pattern of shame, humiliation, rage and becoming invisible. He mutters something.)

Rachel: "Stop muttering." (Albert tears up, which is even more embarrassing for him in front of his friends. Rachel finally gets it that she's publicly humiliating her son, and suddenly remembers his "invisible defense" that was discussed in therapy. She now feels intense shame that she is demeaning Albert, and has an impulse to hug him until she feels better, which is not a superior response in front of his friends. Feeling her anger and shame, she looks at Albert and gets that he's in his overwhelm invisible mode. Disidentifying from her defensive state, she reaches for what will serve the highest good right now. Immediately she has an idea.) "OK boys, come in here and help me clean up the mess." (The three boys troop in, and Rachel starts gathering up her papers and shaking the glass off of them and onto the table. She turns to Albert, who's still shut down, and speaks to him in a caring tone.) "Albert, you know how to clean up glass. Get the broom, dustpan, and rags, and show your friends how to do it. I'm going to take these papers into the office. Oh, and I'm sorry I yelled at you. I was just sitting here and, wham, the window exploded." (She makes a face and a big gesture, and all three boys laugh. Her attunement recruits a complementary state in Albert. He becomes all business.)

Albert: "Sam, you pick up the big pieces and put them in the trash. Aaron, you and I can wipe the table and then sweep the floor."

Rachel: "Good job. We'll have to replace the pane, and you need to pay for some of it."

Albert: (This fits his black and white moral code, and actually helps him let go of the shame of his mistake.) "Sure, Mom, whatever you decide is fair."

Notice how good ideas naturally arise from Rachel's attuned states. We don't need PhD's in development or endless lists of tactics in how to help children grow. All that we need is to feel into ourselves, feel into our children and give each situation our best shot.

What makes this difficult is that stress tends to evoke defensive states. It was stressful to Rachel when her flow state doing taxes was interrupted by Hannah's Barbie crisis. It was stressful to have the baseball come crashing through the window. We get dialed into a state of healthy response, and something happens to lure us into a defensive state. In this example, because of Rachel's sense of responsibility to attune to herself and the kids, none of them spent much time in distressed states, and the initial injuries were quickly repaired. Defensive states were resolved to healthy responses to the present moment. Further, Rachel was not just modeling behaviors, her brain was literally showing their brains how to optimally be in a distressing situation through the mediums of tone, expression, movement, posture, and content.

Quick repair and parental attunement predispose parents and children to spend more time in optimal states of healthy response and less time in defensive states. This reinforces healthy states and the neural networks associated with them. Such "practice" predisposes brains to consolidate attractor states of healthy response, even in stressful situations.

Repair.

The blessing and the burden of being human is that we have a sense of the past, present, and future. This is a blessing because we can accumulate knowledge and wisdom, and anticipate needs and problems. This is a burden because we can lock ourselves in the past and the future in ways that compromise our ability to live in the present moment.

Developmental psychologists, psychotherapists, neuroscientists, and spiritual practitioners all agree that living fully in the present moment is an optimal state of consciousness, often synonymous with being in a state of healthy response. Spiritual teachers such as Eckhart Tolle and David Deida call this "presence."[10] Defensive states pull us out of the present moment into guilt, shame, regret, or rage about the past, or fear, anger, or painful anticipation of the future. How do we deal with defensive states so that we can direct ourselves back to presence? Attunement and repair often result in presence.

Individual repair usually involves some form of disidentifying with a defensive state, and reaching for attunement with self. Rachel felt anger and alarm at Albert, became aware that she was attacking her son, felt shame and an impulse to hug him to make *her* feel better, but instead reached for what might help everybody.

Interpersonal repair involves at least one conflicted partner attuning to self and other with the goal of healthy resolution. Attuning to Albert, feeling his distress, and deciding to normalize the episode and empower him to take charge of cleaning things up gave everybody room to enter positive states of gratitude and felt competence. As the boys were cleaning, Aaron told Albert, "You're Mom's pretty cool. My Dad would have screamed and shouted and grounded me for a week." Hearing this, Albert felt proud of his mother, and became slightly more motivated to cultivate healthy states under stress. His internal working model of a functional adult was incrementally improved. At this point, all involved are showing the signs that repair has happened; affectionate connection, and a sense that justice (the masculine) and compassion (the feminine) have both been served.

Our bodies have evolved to automatically begin repairing physical injury as soon as it happens. We trip and scrape an elbow, and our body immediately mobilizes immune activity and other neurological and physiological processes to deal with physical injury and possible threat. Similarly, we have evolved to initiate automatic repair of psychological and relational injuries.[11] Since our brains are social organs, we are often intimately connected with others in creating and repairing relational injuries. Relationally, repair often looks like seeking and offering help in ways that result in affectionate connection and a sense that justice and compassion are being served.

1. Hawkins (2004)

2. Siegal (2005)

3. Siegal (1999)

4. Kahneman (1999)

5. Wiseman (2003)

6. Siegal (1999)

7. Zinn (2005)

8. Siegal (2005)

9. *Ibid*

10. Tolle (1999)

11. Porges (2006)

5

Repair

Can you think of one person who has grown from infant to adult without physical pain? Can you think of one person who has never experienced emotional pain? Have you ever been in a intimate relationship with a lover, family member, or friend that has been pure pleasure and never involved suffering for either of you?

Life, development, and intimacy all involve regular physical and emotional pain. We cannot prevent much of it; this is necessary suffering. For example, whenever anything unpleasant happens to us, it immediately becomes our responsibility to deal with it; in other words, necessary pain. If a car runs a red light and slams into my truck, the accident was not my fault, but the physical and emotional pains I suffer are my responsibility. I can do my best to heal, grow, and move on with my life, or I can desert myself in response to the emotional injury and physical pain. It's my choice.

As parents it's our responsibility to teach our children how to deal effectively with necessary pain, and to help them learn how to prevent unnecessary suffering. As lovers it's our responsibility to support our partners with their necessary pain and to do our best to avoid causing them unnecessary suffering.

Whether necessary or not, once suffering shows up, it's our responsibility to deal with it. Effectively dealing with pain is one definition of repair.

Defensive states make repair confusing and difficult.

In the last chapter Rachel engaged in effective repair of her own emotional distress when interrupted by Hannah, and shocked by Albert. She helped the children repair their emotional injuries by attuning to them. She felt and accepted Hannah's anger at Emily and Albert's shame and anger at Rachel for publicly chastising him. The process she went through was compassionate acceptance and understanding of what was happening in the present moment, and then consciously reaching for caring action.

This sounds so simple. Compassionate acceptance and understanding of what is happening in the present moment and then consciously reaching for caring action; what's so hard about that? Defensive states are what make repair difficult and demanding. For example, observe what occurs when Harry comes home that afternoon from his golf game:

Harry: (He walks in the door happy, having just spent an enjoyable three hours with his friend Larry playing golf and taking two strokes off his personal best score. He walks into the kitchen and immediately notices that the window has been broken.) "What the hell happened here?"

Rachel: (She's in the other room and is almost done with the taxes. Harry's tone is like fingernails scraping a chalkboard, completely disrupting her flow state.) "I hate it when you come home and start yelling."

Harry: (Now's he's angry at Rachel for "ruining his good mood.") "I'm not yelling! Who broke the God damn window? Was it Albert? I've told him million times to be careful of the house when he's playing in the back yard." (He sees the boys through the back window. They've heard his exchange with Rachel and are looking at each other. Aaron looks at Albert, "Man, you're going to get it." Both Aaron and Sam start getting ready to leave. They want no part of what they anticipate coming. Albert feels frightened and angry and wants to run away. Harry directs his wrath at his son:) "Albert, get in here!"

Rachel: (She's now furious with Harry. She took care of the situation, and it's exploding all over again. In the other room Hannah hears the stress and gets alarmed, "Mommy, I need you." Emily feels the tension in the air, trips on some blocks and hits her head on the couch, and starts to cry. Rachel storms into the kitchen.) "I took care of everything, and then you show up after playing golf all day and start terrorizing everybody. Stop being such a jerk."

Albert: (He walks in on this and has a confusing reaction. He likes his Mom standing up to his Dad, especially to Harry's scary anger, but he feels bad that they're fighting over a mistake he made. Like many children, he tries to deescalate the situation by attacking himself.) "I'm sorry, I'm so stupid. I know you've told me to not throw at the house."

Harry: (He's fully into his defensive state and, even though he's now more angry at Rachel than at Albert, he keeps focused on his son. When Harry was a child, he was verbally humiliated and spanked (sometimes beaten) by both parents when he made mistakes. He would endure these punishments passively or rage against them, creating and practicing neural networks of being a victim or an aggressor when he felt certain kinds of anger, shame, or frustration. Ironically, he prides himself on the fact that he has never physically struck his children, while not realizing how damaging it is when he lashes out with words and tone.) "You're damn right you're stupid. And you're going to pay for this." (His destructive impulse is to get relief by hurting someone, so he attacks his son.) "You're grounded until further notice, and no more playing baseball in the back yard."

Rachel: (She's torn between the two distressed little girls, her emotionally battered son, and her infuriating husband. This overwhelms her capacity for emotional pain and exceeds her window of tolerance. She cycles through shame, humiliation, and rage. When she was a girl, her father and older sister would often attack other family members. The defenses she developed (the altered states and accompanying neural networks she entered and practiced) involved mostly dissociating from her own experience and soothing her family members while secretly despising their cruelty, but occasionally allowing herself to enter destructive rage. Right now she feels fear and contempt toward Harry, but tries to use a soothing tone.) "Now Harry, it's not that bad. I already talked to the kids and took care of it."

Harry: (In his defensive state, he's cut off empathically from Rachel, so he can't feel her efforts to be mature and caring.) "Oh yeah? Well, I don't see a new window. You always undercut me with the kids."

Rachel: (The combination of struggling with the taxes all day, being interrupted regularly by children, the familiar pain of Harry being so "unreasonable and unfair," and the conviction that the current situation is bad for everybody and reflects poorly on her family, is too much to bear.) "Stop it, stop it, stop it! You're being abusive. Get out of here."

Harry: (Now he feels publicly humiliated and overwhelmed. Rachel hardly ever takes this tone with him, and the word "abusive" is one that he particularly hates having applied to him.) "Fine, you won't let me parent, so take care of it yourself." (He storms out of the house, gets in his car, and burns rubber down the street towards his favorite sports bar. Rachel hates it when he drinks too much, and he intends to eat dinner there and have extra drinks just to spite her.)

Rachel: (As he screeches off, she knows he's angrily deserting her and feels hurt at the attack. She's also relieved that he's gone, but sad about how lonely she gets in these situations. Tiredly, she avoids feeling her own pain, and turns to the task of dealing with the upset children.) "OK everybody. Let's all calm down and start cooking dinner."

The above exchange could have gone like this:

Harry: (Walking into the kitchen he sees the window broken and feels distressed and angry.) "Rachel, what happened to the window? Did Albert do it?"

Rachel: (She hears his anger, gets up, walks away from the taxes, and looks Harry's eyes.) "Albert and his friends did it. He felt terrible. I had him clean it up and told him he'd have to pay for part of it."

Harry: (His voice rises as he talks.) "I've told him, if he's going to play baseball in the backyard, that he can't throw at the house. They'll have to play baseball some place else."

Rachel: (She feels a little frustration and fear, but stays connected to herself, Harry, and what she believes is the highest good.) "You're getting upset, and I've already taken care of it. You know our back yard is perfect for pitch and catch. If you want to help, tell him you're proud of him for taking responsibility for his mistake, cleaning up so well, and being fine with paying for it."

Harry: (He's mad and wants to hurt somebody, but feels and accepts this part of himself. He struggles to sooth himself. *"Don't go off on Albert. Rachel hates it and it's bad for him."* He can feel Rachel trying to serve everyone's interests.) "OK, you're right again baby." (She smiles and he senses the pleasure of her appreciation.)

Albert: (As he walks tentatively into the kitchen he anxiously checks out his parents. He's scared of his Dad's capacity to strike out emotionally.) "I broke the window, Dad. I'm sorry. I know you tell me to not throw towards the house. I told Mom I'd pay whatever she said."

Harry: "You're right I've told you about being careful, but I'm proud of the way you're handling it. Your Mom said how you cleaned it up and took responsibility. Mistakes happen, son. We learn from them and go on trying to do right." (Albert relaxes and glows under his father's positive attention. Rachel thinks to herself, *"Harry is such a good father."* Albert's friends are listening outside the broken window. When Albert goes outside, Sam tells him, "Your Dad's cool." Once again, we see the signs that repair has happened; affectionate connection, and a sense in all parties that both justice and compassion are being served.)

Repair begins when we decide to begin it.

There was pain in this alternative scenario, but little unnecessary suffering. There was a lot of unnecessary suffering in the first exchange. The difference between the two is how efficiently Rachel and Harry moved toward repair in the alternate example. As soon as repair becomes a shared agenda, couples who know how to attune make rapid progress.

Rachel and Harry are good-hearted, mostly healthy individuals who never clearly learned their responsibilities for attunement and repair in conflicted intimate relationships. This lack of knowledge and responsibility occasionally leaves them vulnerable.

Since states of consciousness recruit complementary states, two people simultaneously indulging defenses can escalate in a positive feedback spiral that finally explodes into negative dramas such as Rachel kicking Harry out of the house and Harry angrily going to the bar. Here is how we processed the unpleasant scene in therapy two days later:

Keith: (Both Harry and Rachel have just finished describing the situation. They are still visibly angry at each other. Harry came home half drunk Sunday night, and they had another fight, this time fueled by alcohol. Drugs and alcohol are usually explosive, destructive amplifiers of conflict). "It sounds like you two have had a bad couple of days."

Harry: "I said I was sorry. Rachel just can't let it go."

Rachel: "Saying you're sorry doesn't help me deal with Albert and Hannah. It doesn't help my embarrassment having to explain to Emily's mom why she was so upset. It doesn't help me feel any better about you coming home drunk and hassling me again at ten P.M." (Harry looks ashamed, which cues me to interrupt before he can drop deeper into humiliation and rage.)

Keith: "The hard thing about all this is that, instead of taking care of it in minutes, you've been suffering for days. What could you have done differently, Harry?"

Harry: (Masculine people like solving problems. In retrospect while in a state of healthy response, this looks easy to solve.) "I could have not gone off when I got home."

Keith: (*"Challenge him to go deeper."*) "You make it sound so easy. How come you couldn't think of this Sunday?"

Harry: "I was just too mad when I saw that broken window. It drives me crazy when the kids trash the house."

Rachel: (She's still smoldering from two days of emotional turmoil which she blames on Harry, is afraid of letting herself trust Harry again, and is contemptuous of him going off to drink while she was doing the taxes and caring for children.) "You have no idea what it does to the family when you get abusive."

Harry: (Unconsciously slipping into a complementary defensive state where it seems better to attack Rachel than to self-reflect.) "There you go, calling me abusive again. I hate it when you exaggerate."

Rachel: (Self-righteousness is almost always a sign of a defensive state. Feeling morally superior, she turns to me for validation.) "What do you think, Keith? Am I exaggerating?"

Keith: (I look into Harry's eyes and offer him loving challenge.) "I know you were beaten as a child, and you've never laid a hand on any of your children. That means you can control yourself to some extent. When you get angry, like now, can you control what you think and say?" (Harry shifts uncomfortably.)

Harry: "I'm just trying to say what I really feel." (He glares at Rachel.) "Like you're always telling me you want me to do. I do it, and look what happens, you call me abusive." (Rachel gathers herself for a retort, but I interrupt. I want to teach them how to engage in repair, and encourage them to feel responsible to reach for repair when they're distressed.)

Keith: "Saying how you feel when you've surrendered to a defensive state just hurts people. Look at Rachel now. Are you attuned to her? Can you feel into yourself? Are you trying to feel into what it's like to be her? Is your intent, *at this instant*, to serve the highest good?" (Harry looks away.) "Try it. What are you feeling in your body at this moment?"

Harry: (He looks to the left, as people often do when they're monitoring right hemisphere phenomena like bodily sensation or emotion.) "I'm angry and," (He looks surprised.) "worried about Rachel and me."

Keith: "How about you Rachel? What are you feeling in your body?"

Rachel: (We have reduced capacity for effective self-reflection in defensive states. Rachel often blanks out her own experience in conflict.) "I don't know, tense."

Keith: (Rachel often has difficulty discerning nuances of emotion; what neuroscientists call "categorical emotions" like joy, sadness, anger, disgust, surprise, fear, and shame.[1] Like many feminine people, she's learned to respond to conflict by blocking out her own feelings and focusing on others. I help her by giving her choices and letting her respond to them. More feminine people, whether they are men or women, tend to relax when given choices in an accepting environment.[2]) "Is it angry/tense, frightened/tense, sad/tense, or ashamed/tense?"

Rachel: "I'm angry and ashamed that Harry and I act this way."

Keith: "Look at each other, and guess what the other is feeling and wanting."

Harry: "I know you want us to be good, Ratch."

Rachel: (Relaxing hearing his softened tone and his affectionate diminutive of her name.) "You love me and want us to work it out."

Keith: "You notice how automatically you shifted to more positive perspectives when you started feeling into yourselves and each other?" (Both nod.) "When injury happens, you know it because you feel pain and the impulse to attack or desert yourself or your spouse. The quicker you shift your *conscious intent* to attunement and repair, the quicker you get back to love."

Harry: (Like most masculine people, he wants a specific solution.) "How do you repair?"

Keith: "It's different every time because it depends on what you both are feeling and thinking, and what you believe serves the highest good this time. What would you do different if you could go back to Sunday?"

Harry: "I wouldn't get angry at Albert and Rachel."

Keith: "A worthy goal, but probably impossible." (This surprises both of them, which focuses their interest and attention. They are not used to me telling them that positive things are impossible.) "Ninety-nine percent of the time you two will *initially* have the same feelings, thoughts, and impulses you did on Sunday. To be different, you need to notice them and decide to feel into yourself and the other with positive intent, *even though you don't want to do any of those things when you're upset.*"

Harry: (He takes my challenge.) "OK, when I got mad at Albert, I could have taken a deep breath and talked to Rachel before I went off. She's usually a cooler head with the kids."

Rachel: "I could have not told you to leave. I just gave up on us working it out."

Keith: "How do you both feel at this moment?"

Rachel: "Close." (Harry smiles and nods.)

Keith: "A mistake many couples make is that they think they have to talk an issue through to get attuned. I believe that love is best served by attuning first, and then talking about issues. Feel into yourself, feel into the other, and challenge yourself to be more caring. Then talk about an issue, if you still need to."

Harry: "How do we know when an issue is resolved?"

Keith: "Some issues need to be resolved dozens of times in a marriage. Each time, resolution is characterized by affectionate connection and a sense that compassion and justice have both been served. Those are the signs of successful repair."

Rachel: "What a waste these last two days have been. I've felt so bad."

Keith: "Next time, see if you can get back to love in minutes instead of two days. The hardest part is remembering to start repair as soon as someone feels injured. Even if it takes hours, remember to compliment each other on any progress. If you keep getting better at attunement and repair, the sky's the limit."

Rachel: (Like most mothers, and more feminine people in general, she is sensitive to energy and love in her family.) "This didn't work with Brian." (She tears up, thinking of him in Utah.)

Harry: (He reaches out and takes her hand.) "We did the best we could, sweetheart."

Keith: "It's different with kids. Sometimes they cut you off, close down, and have no ability to self-reflect. Then you have to hold onto yourself, do what you believe is best in spite of their lack of active cooperation. On the other hand, this did work for Brian. The school says he'd doing great, and the letter he sent you was so sweet it made both of you cry. You kept working at it for two years until you got him what he needed."

Rachel: (Crying now. This has obviously been a huge added stress to her life.) "I miss him so much."

Harry: "Me too. Brian and I used to have fun, and he was a great older brother to Albert and Hannah when he wasn't being such a jerk."

Rachel: "Harry!"

Harry: (He's suddenly confused.) "What did I say?" (Rather than let him continuing defending himself, I step in.)

Keith: (Laughing.) "We were all in a feel good, love Brian moment, and you called him a jerk." (Now Harry and Rachel start laughing. Harry says, "Oops.")

Keith: "You see, it's not a problem if you notice her distress, resist your impulse to defend, and move to repair. Rachel's good at letting go of anger when you're being your best self. Some wives get so mad that they sometimes can't adjust to affection when their husband starts being excellent."

Rachel: "I've been there a few times." (We laugh again. All three of us are attuned, and everything seems easy.)

Keith: "Remember, notice when you or someone else feels injured and then feel into you, feel into them, and reach for what serves everyone."

Remember what you're about.

I once started writing a book called *Remember What You're About,* but stopped when nobody I described the book to could remember the title. The hardest aspect of repair is to remember to start doing it. This is where our sense of being responsible adults can serve us well. When we truly embrace an adult responsibility, we can often remember it in any circumstance. The fact that Harry had never struck his children is a good example. He remembered this responsibility across a wide range of angry, tired, and overwhelmed states, and there were no exceptions.

Our lives are filled with responsibilities we've embraced: Look both ways before you cross the street, signal before you make a turn, say "thank you" when someone serves you, remember to put your clothes on before you walk outside. The key to embracing a responsibility is to have no loopholes. Say the rule is, "My job is to initiate attunement and repair unless I feel too injured, or too angry, or too overwhelmed, or too anything." Then, in a defensive state, distorted thought will be making a persuasive case as to why this time is an exception. If I feel that my job as a spouse and a parent is to perceive injury and initiate attunement and repair, with no exceptions, then I waste a minimum of time and energy resisting when stressed and remember to initiate attunement and repair when I believe something I did or didn't do has resulted in a family member feeling injured. The more we internalize immediate attunement and repair as *responsibilities*, the more we are great parents to our children and great lovers with our spouse.

What if the other person resists or refuses repair? Relating and handling.

States recruit complementary states. We have genetically programmed predispositions to relate (which requires a felt sense of mutual understanding) and create meaning (which involves telling ourselves an ongoing story about what is happening in our life).[3] If communication is not complementary, we don't have the sense of "being felt" that we crave in relationship, and we'll tell ourselves a story that explains what is happening. In a state of healthy response, our story supports growth and integration. In a defensive state, our story inhibits growth and integration.

When two people are relating, they naturally move towards complementary communication. Presence in one person tends to pull presence in another. Defensive states in one person tend to pull defensive states in another.

When one person is attuned and another is in a defensive state, eventually one or the other will shift. An advantage of attunement is that conscious focus on what everyone is feeling and thinking will inform us when either of us is unable and/or unwilling to shift. In such a case, it's often the best we can do to switch repair strategies from attempting to relate in a collaborative manner to handling the person and the situation. "Handling" refers to implementing unilateral repair strategies without the other necessarily cooperating or even being aware that they are being handled. This happens frequently with kids. The following exchange between Harry and Hannah at the park is an example:

Harry: "Time to go, Hannah. We need to get home for dinner."

Hannah: "I don't want to go. I want to go on the slide some more."

Harry: "All right. Three more slides, and then we go." (Hannah agrees. Three slides later, Harry continues.) "That's three, and now it's time to go."

Hannah: "No, I'm staying at the park."

Harry: (He feels his frustration, and anticipatory distress over being late to dinner. He promised Rachel he'd have Hannah home on time. He feels into Hannah and can sense she's tired, stubborn, and unavailable. He tries to speak in a reasonable, patient tone.) "I'm going to count to three, and if you aren't walking home with me at three, I'm going to carry you. One, two, three." (Hannah starts saying "No, no, no." and, at "three", Harry picks her up and she starts struggling and crying, which is embarrassing for Harry. He gets it that she out of control, and holds her firmly but gently, murmuring:) "I think you're tired and hungry, sweetheart. You'll feel better when we get home to Mommy." (After about fifty steps Hannah relaxes a little and says, "Put me down." Harry gently puts her down and they walk home holding hands.)

Later that night Harry kisses her good night, and tells the story of her day. He explains, "You woke up, and Mommy took you to pre-school. After lunch you and I went to the park and had a lot of fun, especially on the slide. You got tired and hungry, but you liked the slide so much that you wouldn't leave, and I had to count to three and carry you a little ways. Then we got home and had a good dinner."

Initially, Harry had to repair the conflict over the slide with a unilateral intervention. The principle he was following is that you never put distressed, out of control kids in charge of a parent. Later, at bedtime, he initiated collaborative repair by telling Hannah the story of her day and putting her behavior in a context that could help her develop healthy self-reflection.

An example of handling an older elementary school child is the following exchange between Rachel and Albert. which occurred while Hannah was at the park. Albert's been playing video games for two hours, and Rachel walks into the room:

Rachel: "You've been playing video games for two hours. You need to stop and do something else."

Albert: "Just a few more minutes, Mom. I'm almost on level six." (He keeps watching the screen and playing as he talks.)

Rachel: (She can't stand this particular game, *Stealth Ninja Invaders*. The only reason Albert has it in the first place is that he inherited it from Brian. Further, it feels disrespectful for Albert to be talking to her while glued to the screen. She feels her anger and tries to soothe herself, *"He's just a kid, and he loves the game. Use a good tone."*) "Sorry, Albert, you have to stop." (Albert just keeps playing, saying, "Please." Rachel has an impulse to smash the computer, which makes her smile when she notices it. She takes her boundary to the next level.) "Look at me, son." (He reluctantly turns towards her.) "If you don't stop right now, I'm going to have to figure out a boundary and set it. Let's spare both of us. Why don't you go clean your room?" (Albert almost gets it, but notices a Ninja sneaking up on him on the screen and compulsively is back in the game. Rachel takes a deep breath, reaches over and flips off the computer.)

Albert: (Outraged.) "Mom!"

Rachel: "Clean your room, and go outside and do something you enjoy. Then, if you're still mad, we'll talk." (Albert stalks off to his room, grumbling under his breath. Rachel walks back into the kitchen to finish her shopping list, thinking, *"We probably have to give him a ninety minute timer for video games, or I'm going to be doing this every weekend."* She makes a note to herself to talk about the timer idea with Harry, and gets back to work.)

Rachel was feeling into herself and Albert throughout this exchange, and realized that they were telling each other different stories about the situation. Rachel's story was, *"Albert is playing video games too long, and it's my job to redirect him toward healthier activity."* Albert's story was, *"Mom's not letting me do what I want, and that's not fair."* She discerned when relating with him had turned into a useless circular conversation and shifted to handling him. She unilaterally initiated repair immediately when he felt injured by giving him firm direction and then letting go of the incident. Albert, after cleaning his room and walking over to his friend Julian's house to play catch, felt fine and didn't even remember the episode. Rachel's lack of contempt or critical judgment allowed him to glide through the conflict with his dignity intact, and no sense of shame or humiliation. This made him more likely to respond cooperatively the next time, and more able to move forward with his day. If he had later appeared distant or sullen, Rachel would have felt it and initiated collaborative repair. If collaborative repair (relating) once again led into non-productive talk, she would have shifted into unilateral adjustments (handling). This is the endless rhythm of good parenting. We attune, deal with issues collaboratively by relating, and then shift to handling if relating is currently impossible.

Relating with and handling your spouse; similar processes, different responsibilities.

Five days later, Rachel and Harry are in the back yard, doing weekend chores. Rachel isn't consciously aware that her period is due in three days, but she feels crabby and physically uncomfortable. Harry starts pulling nasturtiums from the back of the roses, and she finds it irritating:

Rachel: "Leave them alone! They look nice, and there are more important things to do."

Harry: (He's put off by her preemptory tone, but relates objectively about the issue at hand.) "They'll just take over the flower bed, and it's easier to get them before they explode."

Rachel: "What do you know about gardening? Leave them alone!"

Harry: (He's aware that this is more intensity than the situation warrants. He feels injured and can sense Rachel feeling bad, so he initiates collaborative repair through relating.) "Is there something bugging you? You seem on edge today." (He suddenly suspects that she is pre-menstrual and makes the classic male error of bringing it up while his wife is upset.) "Are you about to have your period?"

Rachel: (This infuriates her.) "What? Every time I get mad at you for making a stupid mistake, I'm PMSing?"

Harry: (Her lack of empathy and quick acceleration let him know he needs to handle her. He's irritated, but he tells himself, *You know she's about due. Use a good tone, and help her relax.*) "I'm sorry. I know you don't like me bringing up the possibility that you're pre-menstrual during an argument. What do you want me to do in the garden?"

Rachel: (She feels somewhat deflated and still has the impulse to go after him, but is rapidly shifting her state of consciousness in response to his caring.) "I really want the weeds in the vegetable garden pulled."

Harry: "Sure, honey." (As he starts pulling the weeds, he smiles slyly over his shoulder at her as she spreads mulch over some flowers.)

Rachel: (She laughs.) "OK. I'm premenstrual, I'm sorry."

In my work with couples, I frequently find myself explaining how, in second stage relationships (and much marriage counseling), the standard is to get back to affectionate connection through mutual processing that is often tedious and exhausting. It is more fun and less work to get to affectionate connection first, and then process if needed. Rather than argue with Rachel about her irritable mood, or passive aggressively do other tasks while telling himself a story about how unreasonable his wife is, Harry felt into himself and Rachel, and initiated repair. He told himself the story that Rachel was PMSing, couldn't immediately relate, and needed some friendly handling. To do this, Harry had to hold on to his irritated self and reach for humor and caring. This pulled a complementary response from Rachel, and repair was accomplished; they had affectionate connection and a sense that compassion and justice were both being served.

Unconditional love in marriage is largely a myth.

I believe that couples should have high standards for repair in their relationships. This reflects the fact that lover relationships, though feeling as if they involve unconditional love, in reality involve the most conditional love there is. In no other relationship do we have the responsibilities to stay positively connected emotionally, intellectually, interpersonally, romantically, and spiritually. If any of these channels are interrupted, injured, or blocked for any length of time *without repair*, the secure sense of love, connection, and attraction that is necessary to be satisfied spouses suffers. Whenever we enter a state of consciousness, we are practicing that state. It's dangerous to allow yourself or your spouse to practice states of consciousness that interfere with love.

On the other hand, if spouses become progressively more adept at discerning injury and initiating (and responding positively to) efforts at repair, love and passion tend to grow. We spend progressively more time in healthy states where we feel loving, appreciative, attractive, and attracted. This is one explanation of the fact that some couples report having the best sex of their lives in their fifties and sixties;[4] they have gradually improved their relating, attuning, and repair skills over many years, resulting in deepening erotic polarity and better skills in loving.

Individual repair.

You'll notice in all the above examples, attunement and repair begins with an adult dealing effectively with interior pain. This doesn't mean children can't initiate repair; children initiate repair all the time. "I'm sorry, Mommy," "Daddy, I feel bad," "Aunt Josie, I don't like it when you're mad at me," "What's wrong, Mommy?" "Daddy, I had a bad day," are all common examples. These are usually moments of healthy response where a child identifies internal distress and appropriately seeks help from a competent adult. One definition of healthy development could be increasing frequency of these moments in a child's life until he or she becomes a competent adult who feels responsible for everything they experience and do, including responsibility to initiate repair when somebody feels injured.

We tend to parent ourselves the way we were parented. If we were appropriately responded to by our parents, we internalize their voices and presence to learn how to appropriately respond to ourselves as infants, toddlers, elementary schoolers, teenagers, and adults. In the absence of such training, we can decide to learn how to care more effectively for ourselves. Being responsive and caring to our own pain is individual, or internal, repair.

First, accept what is.

Internal repair begins with accepting what is. I feel anxious, angry, ashamed, guilty, hurt, embarrassed, sad, helpless, weak, unattractive, powerless, or in physical pain, and I accept myself and my experience.

Over the years, many of my clients have come into therapy wanting to rid themselves of aspects they fear or despise. This is the cosmetic surgery attitude toward therapy.

I wish it were that easy or even possible to excise destructive aspects of ourselves. I have no problem with a client wanting to get rid of her anxiety, depression, or capacity for critical judgment. Unfortunately, human brains don't work that way. We never lose our capacity to be in any state we've practiced. My clients often suffer because they fight against inner experience instead of accepting, processing, and integrating it. I usually tell them, "We can, and should, learn how to change states of consciousness. It's good that you identify different states that you want to change. Let's explore what states you want to spend more time in and learn how to practice them."

Development is include and transcend, not dissociate and transcend, deny and transcend, or execute and transcend. We have in us the baby crying for the breast, the toddler wanting the world to organize around his or her egocentric desires, the child who believes all should obey black and white rules, and the teen who challenges authority. In addition, we all have a feminine aspect that yearns for love and fullness and a masculine aspect that craves freedom and emptiness. We are each a community of selves that is either more coherent and healthy, or more rigid and/or chaotic. Health is improving our abilities to accept all aspects of who we are and organizing them to live healthy, productive lives.

As we accept what is, we can more effectively practice internal attunement. What am I feeling, thinking, and wanting, and what serves the highest good? If I can accept what is, it helps liberate me to identify and commit to doing what feels right at this moment. Steven Hayes has a whole system of psychotherapy, called ACT (Acceptance and Commitment Therapy) based on these simple principles.[5] Internal repair always involves these practices either consciously or unconsciously. In the above examples of effective repair, Harry needed to accept his anger at Hannah for throwing a tantrum and his impulse to critically judge Rachel for yelling at him. Rachel had to accept her desire to smash Albert's computer and her angry attack on Harry for wanting to weed the "wrong" flowerbed.

Internal repair begins with accepting what is and then organizing our inner experience to make compassionate sense. This is an integrative process that helps organize our inner community into a more complex and effective whole. This drive for freer flow of energy and more efficient information processing characterizes human brain development. What blocks this natural developmental flow is defensive states where we resist awareness of, acceptance of, and responsibility for painful aspect of ourselves. The following is an internal process that Brian is going through in Mountain View School in Utah after four months of mostly positive progress. He was caught smoking a stolen cigarette and has been told he needs to talk to his group about what he did. He's on restriction, sitting in his room with the direction to consider what his rule breaking might be about. His inner dialog is:

> Brian: *"Fuck them. It's just a cigarette, it's not like I smoked pot, or did speed or anything."* (He stares out his widow at the high desert that surrounds the school, and remembers what he's been learning.) *"Come on. You stole a cigarette and then lied about it. Of course they're going to do something. Your bunkmates have a consequence because you did it. They need to have a special meeting."* (Now he feels ashamed.) *"You asshole. This is just like you. Things were going great and you screwed it up."* (He remembers his counselor telling

him to not call himself an asshole.) *"Gary's right. You did this for a reason. What was it? Maybe the group can help me figure it out. I'll ask them."* (His suspicion that there is some hidden meaning to his mistake and his decision to ask the group for help are soothing to him. He feels both relief and pride. He senses this position will be well received, and now feels a small tingle of positive anticipation of discussing the episode, combined with a sense of fairness about his consequence.)

At this point, Brian is having the experience of effective internal repair; a feeling of affectionate connection (or acceptance) of himself, combined with a sense that compassion and justice are being served. This individual repair sets him up to engage in relational repair with his housemates, who have had to endure their own consequences from his rule breaking.

Repair is a necessary aspect of attunement.

Consistent attunement is impossible without the ability and willingness to engage in *intra*personal and *inter*personal repair. Feeling into myself will regularly involve encountering painful feelings, distorted thoughts, and destructive impulses that are my responsibility to deal with. Denial, blame, suppression, and self-flagellation all lead to more pain and distortion. Acceptance and reaching for right action leads to emotional growth and clarity of thought. Feeling into another person will occasionally lead to discovering that he or she feels injured in some fashion. Once again, defense, blame, rejection, or attack lead to more problems. Acceptance and reaching for right action lead to healthy relating or handling. In our intimate relationships with our children and spouse, initiating repair in the presence of injury is almost always a good idea.

1. Siegal (1999)

2. Deida (2004)

3. Siegal (2003)

4. Schnarch (1997)

5. Hayes (1999)

6

Attuning to Babies

My friend Denton Roberts, a gifted therapist and minister, once told me that if you wait till you're ready to have children, you'll wait forever, because no one is ever completely ready to have children. Parenting makes you ready for parenting. An unfortunate fact of western childrearing is that we are most inexperienced as parents when our infant children are the most vulnerable and sensitive to our parenting. On the other hand, recent research has also shown that one weekend of training in how to care for and relate to newborns can reduce post-partum depression rates from sixty percent to thirty percent in women, and thirty percent to fifteen percent in men.[1] This suggests that parents can benefit enormously from relatively little input. It also suggests that adults are constitutionally primed to help babies thrive.

Babies are learning machines whose brains are growing at a phenomenal rate. One third of our genes are devoted exclusively to neural development, and one sixth are devoted indirectly.[2] That's *one half* of our genes dedicated to establishing, guiding and maintaining our developing neural networks. On the other hand, much genetically driven neural development is guided by ongoing experience. Babies' brains grow in response to their interactions with the environment, and, especially, their social environments with mother, father, and other primary caregivers. How parents attune to babies literally guides the development of babies' nervous systems.[3]

There have been wonderful studies done on how parents' manner of relating, or *attachment style,* has direct influence on babies' attachment style. A fascinating outcome of this research is that, even though we are genetically programmed to relate to, bond with, and care for babies, and we are all born with different temperaments, attachment style seems relatively independent of genetic and congenital (what happened to us in the womb) predisposition. This is reflected in the facts that babies can have a secure attachment style with one caregiver, and an insecure attachment style with another caregiver, that parental attachment style is a reliable predictor of infant attachment style even with adopted children, and that people can change their attachment style at any time throughout life. In other words, no matter what temperament our baby is born with (harm avoidant, novelty seeking, dependent, persistent, self-directed, self-transcendent, cooperative, and distractible are all examples of genetic and/or congenital temperamental predispositions[4]), their attachment style will be largely a function of attunement with primary caregivers. The overwhelming determinant of how successfully an infant relates is how successfully a parent relates, *and parents can improve their attachment styles by learning and practicing successful relating, or when they otherwise choose to develop more coherent life narratives.*[5]

Secure attachment.

Secure attachment is the optimal attachment style in parents and infants.[6] What attachment researchers call a secure autonomous attachment style in an adult is reflected in a coherent sense of their life story. All that they've experienced makes sense in the person they are, and they have a positive conception of moving forward into the future.[7]

A secure attachment style in an infant is reflected in babies that can reach confidently for a reliably caring parent when baby needs contact and can create comfortable separation when baby needs separation. Secure attachment has proven to be a relatively stable personality trait that has been associated with greater emotional, cognitive, and social health. Fifty-five to sixty-five percent of children have secure attachment.[8]

An important aspect of a secure attachment style is that it can be acquired at any time in our lives. People who had insecure attachment styles as infants and then developed secure attachment styles by adulthood almost all report their transformation to be a result of an intimate relationship with a family member, lover, teacher, or friend. At some point, their life story changed from a chaotic or rigid one to a coherent narrative where their life made sense in the past and had a positive direction toward their future. Parents find this data reassuring. We don't have to inflict past traumas on our children. Even if we've had a sub-optimal childhood ourselves, or have difficulty with our own relationships, we can decide to learn and practice attunement to develop a coherent life narrative and help our children have optimal attachment styles.

Interestingly, attachment style seems to be relatively independent of genetic predisposition or temperament. Almost all other aspects of personality are affected by temperamental factors such as harm avoidance, novelty seeking, dependence, persistence, self-directedness, self-transcendence, and cooperativeness.[9] Personality researchers have found that secure and insecure attachment seem to be, as far as they can determine, functions of interactional style, independent of temperament.[10]

As was mentioned in Chapter One, clinician and researcher John Gottman suggests that being accessible and responsive (what attachment researchers call "contingent") thirty percent of the time is enough attunement for a baby to establish secure attachment. Let's return to Jim and Sally, the couple we met in Chapter One, ten months after the birth of their second baby, Eric:

> Eric: (It is eleven A.M. Wednesday morning and Eric has just woken from his morning nap. He's alone in his crib and his diaper is wet and somewhat uncomfortable. He starts to cry mildly. It's not urgent, but he wants contact and comfort.)

> Sally: (She's just sitting down with a cup of coffee to read the paper. Jim's at work, Jake's at preschool, and the past hour since Eric went down has been a whirlwind of dishes, laundry, and picking up the house (I have never seen a house where small children live that, to some extent, wasn't constantly in disarray). She feels a flash of frustration, but relaxes and takes another sip of coffee. She can hear that Eric isn't in real distress, so she gathers herself and reluctantly puts down the paper, while calling out to her son.) "Coming Eric." (She walks into his room, and he immediately reaches out to her and makes a slightly more urgent sound.) "Did you have a nice nap? I'll bet you're wet. Let's see and change you." (As she picks him up she expertly checks him, and then puts him down on the changing table as she smiles and coos. He smiles and coos back. She changes him, and caries him into the living room where there are toys and a day crib. He roots around for her breast, but she's in the process of teaching him how to sleep through the night (she following the plan outlined in Suzy Giordano's excellent book, *Twelve Hours' Sleep by Twelve Weeks Old*[11]), so she distracts him with bouncing him on her knee and singing the Itsy Bitsy Spider. After about fifteen minutes, she lets him nurse for about seven minutes until he's full. She burps him, and notices how he's looking away at different objects in the room. She puts him in his day crib under a musical mobile and walks to the other side of the room to do some ironing.)

Eric has secure attachment with Sally. When he needs contact, he indicates it and contact shows up. When he wants separation, he indicates it by looking away and Sally supports separation. When he needs boundaries (like postponing his nursing for fifteen minutes in response to the protocols in *Twelve Hours Sleep by Twelve Weeks Old*), Sally provides boundaries. Even though he has little or no conscious memory at this age (conscious, explicit memory begins to show up around eighteen months) his brain and body are learning and growing. If this rhythm of attuned contact, separation, and boundaries is maintained, Eric, in the absence of trauma, will literally absorb a sense of a caring presence into his nervous system; what attachment researchers call an inner working model. This inner sense of a stable, caring presence endures while Sally is present or absent and will become a source of self-confidence and secure attachment with others in later life.

This all seems so simple and self-evident. What can possibly go wrong? How can a parent not notice and respond to a baby's need for contact, separation, and boundaries thirty percent of the time? Just ask any parent. Sometimes attunement to self and infant seems like the hardest thing on earth.

Insecure attachment.

Parenting our children begins with how we care for ourselves. Just as adults with secure/autonomous attachment styles tend to raise infants with secure attachment styles, research has shown that certain forms of insecure adult relating styles predispose infants to insecure attachment patterns. The three major insecure attachment combinations are dismissive adult and avoidant infant, preoccupied adult and ambivalent (or resistant) infant, and unresolved/disorganized adult and disorganized/disoriented infant.

People are complex, and most parents and infants have unique combinations of various attachment styles, as well as bad days and stressed moments where nobody is behaving optimally. This is normal development. Often, though, the predominant pattern between parent and infant constellates into secure adult/secure infant, dismissive adult/avoidant infant, preoccupied adult/ambivalent infant, or unresolved and disorganized adult/disorganized and disoriented infant (usually the unresolved/disorganized pair also includes predominantly one of the other insecure attachment patterns). The three insecure attachment combinations are all driven, in one form or another, by a parent's difficulties with attunement.

Dismissive adult and avoidant infant.

Dismissive adult attachment means that an individual's predominant relating style in intimacy is denial, repression, suppression, or avoidance of emotion in themselves and others. Adults who engage in this style of relating tend to raise infants who learn to not seek comfort from adults, but instead tend to repress emotion and keep to themselves. If Sally and Eric had a dismissive/avoidant attachment style, the above exchange might have looked like this:

Eric: He wakes and cries.

Sally: She hears him and thinks to herself, *"I just got my cup of coffee. Let him cry it out."*

Eric: His crying gets more urgent, but Sally is reading the paper and tuning him out. Finally, he gets tired and quiets down a little.

Sally: She's done with her coffee, and walks into his room. He sees her, but barely reacts. She picks him up and changes him without speaking.

All of us have had episodes somewhat like this with our babies, but, if this is the standard emotional relationship between a primary caregiver and infant, the child is likely to learn to not rely on a parent for what attachment researchers call a "safe haven" or "secure base,"[12] and will often develop an emotionally repressed, controlling personality that is unpopular with other children. Such a child is more likely to grow into an adult who tends to deny, repress, suppress, or avoid emotional experience and expression.[13]

Preoccupied adult and resistant or ambivalent infant.

Preoccupied adult attachment means that an individual's predominant relating style in intimacy is inconsistent, distracted, and unduly influenced by internal states and intrusions from the past.[14] This can result in relating that's regularly characterized by reduced empathy; often driven more by personal impulse than by attunement to another. Parents with a preoccupied attachment style don't consistently give babies the contact they crave when they want it, push unwanted contact on babies in the face of signals that they don't want it, and impose boundaries that are more arbitrary, inconsistent, and impulsive, instead of consistent, thoughtful, and contingent (based on what an infant is indicating he or she needs). This tends to influence children to be clingy, not easily soothed, anxious, and demanding. If Sally and Eric had a preoccupied/ambivalent attachment style, their exchange might have looked like this:

Eric: He wakes, cries a little and then calms down and starts sucking his thumb.

Sally: She hears the initial cry, rushes into the room, does not notice that Eric has soothed himself, and hugs him to her breast saying, "Poor baby, poor baby."

Eric: Somewhat shocked by Sally's handling, starts to whimper and struggle a little.

Sally: Eric resisting her hug creates an association with how her mother didn't like to be hugged when Sally was a little girl. Even though there is no conscious sense of something being remembered, Sally engages the neural network that she practiced endlessly with her mother, and enters an irritated and anxious state. She holds Eric up in front of her and says, "What's wrong? I picked you up."

Eric: The reproach in Sally's tone feels bad to him and he starts crying, leading Sally to feel more inept and frustrated. She impulsively opens her blouse and gives him her breast. He settles down and starts nursing. Three minutes later, the phone rings, and Sally, unthinking, pulls him off her breast, saying, "That's enough for now," while she carries him into the kitchen to answer the call from her friend Julie. Eric starts to fuss and grab at Sally's breast, and she whisks him into his crib while talking into the phone.

Julie: "What's wrong? I hear Eric crying."

Sally: "He's just fussy today."

Once again, all parents are preoccupied and not attuned to their baby on occasion. If this is the predominant relating style, children grow up not having the sense of being "felt" by parents. They are likely to have the experience of being regularly intruded upon when they need separation (as Eric was when he was effectively self-soothing in his crib, and Sally swept him up with "Poor baby"), or being ignored when they need contact (Sally stopping nursing before Eric was done, not burping him, and not attending to his distress while she was talking to Julie). This attachment style can result in babies growing into anxious adults who have difficulty self-reflecting, self-soothing, and consistently feeling into others.

Unresolved/disorganized adult and disorganized/disoriented baby.

Allan Schore, in a conference at UCLA in March of 2006, suggested that dissociation rather than repression might be the basis of most defensive systems.[15] This was a bold statement since repression of conflicted material has been assumed to be the central feature of many psychological problems since the time of Freud.[16]

Repression is unconsciously pushing unwanted, painful, or forbidden material away from awareness. Dissociation is a different, though related, process, where, if there is too much subjective distress associated with an event, it is processed in our implicit memory but is blocked from our conscious, explicit memory. In other words, our brains and bodies register an event and our defensive reaction to it, but when we are affected by the learning that occurred as a result, there is no conscious sense that something is being remembered.[17] Since our brain's initial appraisal of the event was that it was too emotionally charged to focus conscious attention on, we have instinctive fear of bringing such material into self-reflective awareness, and we thus resist integrating our implicit memory with our conscious, explicit memory. This leaves us vulnerable to flashbacks, or associations that can be distressing and highly emotional, but in which there is no conscious sense of being affected by past events. In the preoccupied example with Sally, she had no idea that Eric's resistance to her hug evoked an association with her rejecting mother. All Sally felt was anxious irritation at Eric, which she reflexively avoided examining. If she had learned and practiced effective self-reflection, this pattern could have long since been confronted and changed.

We can dissociate in response to extreme negative arousal. A caregiver that is either terrifying or terrified can evoke terror in an infant, often causing the child's stress response to be overwhelmed and react with protest, confusion, or immobilization. Adults with unresolved trauma can be stimulated by environmental cues to enter overwhelming states of distress. Post traumatic stress reactions to horrifying events such as abuse, life threatening situations, or subjectively terrifying experiences can be cued by otherwise benign environmental conditions and involve extreme defensive reactions.[18] Like most defensive reactions, there is often little inclination or ability to effectively self-reflect on these restimulations.

Adults in the grip of terrifying states (often involving rage, terror, intense shame, or horror) can be terrifying to infants, who rely on attunement with caregivers for soothing and self-regulation. Infants' brains are programmed to turn to a parent for comfort when feeling distress. When the caregiver is the *source* of extreme distress, the child's neural networks can be short circuited, resulting in "frozen," ineffectual responses that can become hard wired neural circuits. These circuits can involve varying degrees of dissociation under stress, and negatively affect brain development. If Sally and Eric had an unresolved/disorganized attachment style, their exchange might have looked like this:

Jim: He has just come home for lunch and, after picking up Eric and kissing him, sits down at the table with Sally, and they both start to read the paper. He sees a headline on page three, *Girl raped by brother*. This reminds him of

Sally's three month sexual relationships with her older brother Sam, when she was ten, and he becomes furious. Even though the relationship was consensual and Sam stopped it because he felt too guilty and ashamed, Jim despises Sam for it, has never resolved his anger, and blames the episode for all his and Sally's sexual problems. These problems are surfacing more at this point because, even though Sally has largely recovered physically from the birth, she, like many nursing mothers, has reduced libido due to fatigue and hormonal shifts. "Here's another brother who abused his sister."

Sally: She has always felt intense shame over the sexual involvement with her brother, and can't stand to think about it. She feels a curious blankness now as she hears the story, and doesn't want to discuss it. "Leave it alone Jim." She doesn't notice that Eric is crying until it's gone on for several minutes. She goes in to change him with a blank look on her face. Eric does not feel "felt" by blank-faced Sally and becomes scared. As she opens his diaper, a jet of urine shoots out and splatters her blouse. This is reminiscent enough of some episodes with Sam that, horrified, she screams, "NO, stop it!"

Eric: Terrified, he starts to scream and thrash around. Sally looks at him with scary eyes and yells, "Stop it!" This is too much negative emotional intensity for Eric, and he freezes and looks away toward the corner of the room.

If this interaction were characteristic of Sally and Eric's relationship, her unresolved issues would keep creating these frightening episodes that would influence Eric to form a disorganized/disoriented attachment style. This added to either an avoidant or ambivalent style, would likely result in Eric having insecure attachment and an increased capacity for dissociation under stress.

What to do? Practice attunement.

There are many outstanding books on parenting. My current favorites on parenting infants are Dan Siegal's and Mary Hartzell's *Parenting from the Inside Out* and Suzy Giordano's *Twelve Hours Sleep by Twelve Weeks Old*. These and similar books capture the essence of parenting infants while increasing your capacities to hold on to yourself. All of them agree that there are no perfect parents, no perfectly happy babies, and that we need to work on ourselves to be better parents.

Life is messy. All parents have dismissive, preoccupied, or unresolved moments. How we process these moments determines our attachment style and powerfully influences our children's development. If we deny, suppress, blame, attack, or collapse into shame or guilt, *without initiating attunement and repair,* we are dramatically less likely to learn from distressing episodes and more likely to repeat them. If, *as we experience* emotional pain, distorted thoughts, and destructive impulses, we can self-reflect enough to reach for attunement and repair, we grow individually and support healthy attachment in our children.

Infants are born relating and never stop. Their brains and bodies are always communicating in one form or another. A key to attuning to babies is noticing when we're "listening" to their experience. When I become so distressed, distracted, fatigued, or upset, that I stop paying attention to what my baby is "saying" and I simply notice this and reach to attune, good things start happening.

In the above examples, Sally could initiate attunement and repair at any time during or after the incidents. Repair with infants begins with parents getting hold of themselves. By cultivating self-reflection, refusing to indulge distorted thoughts and destructive impulses, and reaching for empathetic connection, we have many options instead of the compulsive distressed alternatives that we feel locked into in defensive states.

Supporting your love affair with your spouse while attuning to your infant.

Infants are adorable, and creating a family is one of the most meaningful experiences that many of us will ever have. Nevertheless, infants tend to stress marital relationships.[19] As I tell parents, "We don't have kids for the money or the stress reduction."

Pregnancy and childbirth involve huge changes for mothers and fathers. Some women feel less physically attractive as pregnancy advances, and some men feel less attracted when their lover becomes a mother. These difficulties can continue after delivery because of fatigue, hormonal changes cued by nursing and the presence (sight, sound, smell, and touch) of an infant, genital pain, painful associations with the genital area, or by weight gain during pregnancy. Childbirth is exhausting and can be emotionally traumatic for everyone involved. The responsibilities and demands of caring for an infant can be overwhelming. Testosterone levels go down significantly in both men and women in the later stages of pregnancy and in the presence of infants.[20] This potentially reduces libido in both partners.

Sexual contact often becomes somewhat of a distant memory during this period. Explicit talk about sex is rarely taught and generally discouraged in our culture, so even parents with secure/autonomous attachment styles can find themselves alienated from their lover and inhibited discussing feelings and needs. Similarly, erotic polarity, and the nature and responsibilities of being a more feminine or more masculine partner in a love affair are alien concepts to many, and even politically offensive to second stage, egalitarian worldviews. This makes erotic polarity particularly vulnerable to disruptions, since repair is often compromised by deep-seated inhibitions around even discussing sexual needs and issues.

It's easy for the parents' love affair to get lost in all these changes and demands.

Chapter Two introduced sexual polarity, and feminine/masculine principles and practices. Jim and Sally's therapy session ten months after Eric's birth was presented as an example of initiating repair in the presence of typical injuries that arise during childbirth and infant care. Erotic polarity doesn't necessarily require physical intercourse to be supported in a marriage. It does seem to require maintenance and repair to be sustained as a relational foundation during times of change, such as pregnancy, birth, and adjusting to parenthood.

Simply knowing the responsibilities of a masculine or feminine partner and attuning with the goal of supporting erotic polarity can be reassuring. In Sally and Jim's session, Sally's yearning for romance and eroticism was comforting to Jim, *when she made it visible.* Jim's attraction to Sally and desire to reestablish their love affair was comforting to Sally, when neither of them was blaming or pathologizing themselves or each other for the problems they were having. The following is an exchange that happened forty minutes into the session:

Jim: "I don't know what you mean when you say I need to help Sally feel known and claimed, and safe and loved."

Keith: "Sally, what's Jim like when you're feeling affectionate and attracted to him?"

Sally: "I love it when he's sweet with the kids. I like it when he notices I'm tired or distracted and helps out. I like it when he asks me about my day and really listens."

Jim: "OK, but what about sex?"

Sally: (She looks disgusted.) "It's all about sex to you, isn't it?" (Jim looks angry and ashamed.)

Keith: (I want them to interrupt their relational defensive pattern and attune.) "Feel into yourselves right now and look at each other. What's happening?"

Jim: "We're starting our same old argument."

Keith: "What's your part of it, Jim?"

Jim: (Speaking slowly, as he works to understand himself and not attack Sally.) "I'm pushing Sally to be sexual. I don't really trust that being good with the kids and attentive and helpful will really make sex better."

Sally: "I don't want to trade sex for you being nice."

Keith: "Sally, feel into yourself and Jim. What's your part of the pattern?"

Sally: (There are too many personal and cultural blocks in this area for Sally to have a clear sense of the pattern she's in. All she feels is confusion, but, since she also feels safe at this moment and wants love to work in her family, she also has some curiosity as to what her part might be.) "I don't know. What do you think?"

Keith: "You've been taught to resist conscious awareness of your sexual nature and needs. You said you'd like enough sleep, more romance in your life, and that you feel more attracted to Jim when he's good with the kids and attentive to you."

Sally: (Laughing.) "You're right. I already forgot that I said that stuff."

Keith: "So what happens if Jim's doing those attractive things, chooses a moment when you have a little time and energy, and approaches you playfully, the way you've told him pleases you?"

Sally: "I guess I'd like it."

Keith: "Twenty minutes later, while you're making love, do you think you'd be having a good time, and feel that you were creating more love in your marriage?"

Sally: "Definitely."

Jim: (Exasperated.) "That's what I've been saying." (Sally shuts down and looks away in response to his critical tone. Jim gathers himself for another attack, but I interrupt him in the way I want him to interrupt himself.)

Keith: "Jim, you've lost your connection with yourself and Sally."

Jim: (He wakes up a little to what he's doing.) "I get it. I'm sorry sweetheart. I know you hate it when I get critical and impatient."

Sally: (She relaxes a little and looks at him.) "You don't know how hard it is with the baby."

Jim: "I know, but you're great with him and Jake. I know I need to be more patient and not let my temper get the better of me."

Keith: "Sally, is Jim more or less attractive at this moment?"

Sally: "Definitely more attractive."

Keith: "So, show him your pleasure through your body." (Sally impulsively reaches over and caresses his cheek. Jim becomes instantly tender. There is suddenly a palpable attraction between them.) "Put together enough moments like this, and gradually you start discovering how to be lovers while you have an infant and a little boy in the house."

Attuning to an infant and then to your spouse is a lot like singing a lullaby and then shifting into singing a ballad. Accomplished singers can do this routinely because they know how to sing both songs and they've practiced shifting from one to the other. Learning to consciously attune to your infant and your spouse, and practicing shifting focus back and forth as the moment demands, results in being a great parent to your children and a great lover to your spouse.

1. Gottman (2005)

2. Johnson (2005)

3. Siegal (2005)

4. Cloniger (2004)

5. Siegal (2003)

6. Bowlby (1988)

7. Siegal (1999)

8. Siegal (2005)

9. Cloniger (2004)

10. Siegal (2005)

11. Giordano (2006)

12. Bowlby (1988)

13. Siegal (1999)

14. *Ibid*

15. Shore (2006)

16. Freud (1949)

17. Siegal (1999)

18. van der Kolk (2005)

19. Gilbert (2006)

20. Lemonick (2004)

7

Our Violence Can Help Us Be Better Parents and Lovers

We are born with the innate capacities to do violence to self and others and innate responses to the experience of being a victim of violence.[1] In this book, I'm defining different aspects of violence very specifically. Violence to myself is when I seek relief by injuring myself physically or psychologically. Violence to another is when I seek relief by injuring another physically or psychologically. I become a victim of violence when circumstances (like a car accident) or another's actions (for example, if you strike me or scream at me) result in my brain activating the neural circuits that say "I am victim of violence" with corresponding cognitive, emotional, endocrine, and neurological reactions. How we process a violent experience determines how effectively we integrate the traumatic event into a coherent sense of our life story or personal narrative.[2] In general, attunement is an optimal strategy for processing violence.

The tendencies to do violence, and our natural responses when we interpret ourselves to be victims of violence, are important capacities, hard wired through our genetic programming to motivate us to do right by our own standards (which we generally feel we share with personally important social groups) and to defend ourselves from threat.

Let's briefly examine the importance of being able to do violence to others. You are walking down a dark street and are accosted by a man demanding your wallet. You become angry and frightened, and you scream, shout, and push him away. He runs down an alley, and you feel a sense of triumph. You sought and felt relief by attacking your assailant. As the French trauma researcher Pierre Janet established early in the first part of the last century, you resolved this traumatic event by progressing through it to a sense of triumph.[3] You are certainly alarmed by your experience, and probably will become more gun shy walking alone at night, but are unlikely to develop an unresolved sense of post-traumatic stress

89

because you appropriately activated your self-protective capacity for violence and used it to engage in moral activity to a sense of triumph. It felt "right" to protect yourself by attacking this man, and you successfully attacked him until you felt resolved.

Similarly, violence to self has its roots in our need to be socially cooperative beings. The capacity to attack ourselves helps us establish position on personally important social hierarchies by enforcing our internalized standards of those hierarchies. These standards involve a felt sense of shared morality; subjectively, an understanding about what is good and bad that we believe we have in common with our communities.[4] For example, imagine you are shopping at the supermarket and munching on a candy bar as you push your cart down the aisles. At the checkout, the cashier misses adding the candy to your bill, and you hesitate to remind him to charge you. As you pause, a wave of guilt washes over you, and you think, *"You jerk, don't steal."* At this point you tell him that you ate a candy bar and should be charged. As he rings it up, you feel a sense of relief and moral satisfaction that you did the right thing. Calling yourself a "jerk" was a form of violence to self that felt right because it translated into insisting on being "good" when you had an impulse to be transgressive, or "bad."

Violence that doesn't feel morally justified, does not resolve into a sense of triumph, or that leaves us normalizing being a victim or a victimizer, tends to interfere with healthy development.[5] Bullies in elementary school are more likely to have been victims of physical violence and are more likely to have academic problems, legal problems, and relationship problems in later life. Chronic victims tend to develop relational styles where they unconsciously evoke abuse and then resist it ineffectually.[6]

Aggression has been studied exhaustively by biological and social scientists. Frustration leads to aggression,[7] modeling aggression teaches aggression,[8] and a history of being victimized increases the chances for future victimization and future aggression.[9]

Aggression and violence are related but distinct entities. Opponents can battle aggressively in the boxing ring, the martial arts studio, the tennis court, the card table, or the boardroom, but not be seeking relief by hurting each other. I can feel regret at making a mistake, or be frustrated by my inability to solve a problem, without seeking relief by hurting myself. Violence, as it is defined here, involves inflicting suffering for relief.

When emotional and/or physical violence is a result of defensive states, it can be egocentric and selfish in that there is little or no care or empathy for the object of the violence. In these situations there is rarely a compassionate sense that this violence serves the highest good, but instead, if we are the perpetrator, can involve moral outrage ("You deserve this") and/or sadistic entitlement ("I do this because I want to") that justifies the attacks. In such cases there is often a sense of relief from feeding off of the victim's pain. This relief can involve satisfaction at seeing a look of hurt on another's face as we injure them or satisfaction at characterizing ourselves in insulting, demeaning ways when we violate our personal moral code.

Violence is something we all experience, in one form or another, on a daily basis; especially psychologically. I've found most people to be unaware of much of the psychological violence they perpetrate and endure. Strangely, understanding, caring for, and integrating our violent side, and compassionately understanding and handling others' violence, are often necessary components of health, love, and erotic polarity.

Development is include and transcend.

As we explored in Chapter Three, we are always in flux on a variety of developmental lines including how we think, relate, make moral decisions, and process our emotions. Most of us grow from being primarily egocentric as babies and small children, to being primarily conformist/ethnocentric (identifying and caring exclusively for our family, tribe, or nation) as school age children, toward being more worldcentric as adults. As we develop, we don't lose the capacities and impulses that we've had, we include them in larger selves with more capacities.[10] In interpersonal neurobiological terms, we tend to move toward greater response flexibility where we have access to an increasing range of alternatives and better ability to make optimal choices in different situations.[11]

All mammals have the capacity and tendency toward violence in emotionally charged situations, and humans are no exceptions. Part of socialization is internalizing group standards in learning to not lash out *inappropriately* at another in rage or rend ourself *inappropriately* in anger or despair. Different cultures and individuals have different standards of what's appropriate. Sometimes these standards are at odds with how we really function.

When we don't live up to the standards we believe are right, we can experience a distressing dissonance that can lead to shame, denial, dissociation, and an inability to effectively self-reflect, depending on how well attuned we are at that moment. If my family taboos say it is forbidden to feel rage, or an impulse to hurt another, whenever I have those experiences I might plunge into a distressing dissonance of not living up to my moral standards. Possible reactions to such dissonance are denial ("I'm not angry, and I have no impulse to attack"), dissociation ("what just happened?"), violence to self ("I'm an awful person"), or attunement. An example of attunement might be, "I'm angry and have impulses to attack, and I feel shame which suggests I'm finding these natural human reactions to be unacceptable. Since I consciously know that feelings and impulses are innocent and should be accepted, considered, and integrated rather than rejected and pathologized, I need to widen my range of acceptable experiences to include anger and impulses to attack others." Such self-reflective activity often results in a sense of satisfaction, or triumph, at the resulting transformative insights. The experience of affectionate connection with self combined with a sense that compassion and justice are being served are signature qualities of internal repair. This process of differentiation of an aspect of self through awareness and self-reflection and integration through acceptance and transformative insight is consistent with most psychotherapeutic systems.[12]

The impulse is not the act.

Since we tend to parent ourselves the way we were parented (as infants we internalize parental presences as internal working models of how to deal with the world[13]), we often tend to relate to our violent selves the way our parents did. If you were shamed for raging and hitting your sister when you were a toddler, you will tend to shame yourself for raging, hitting, *or impulses to rage or hit* as a child, adolescent, and adult. Since our minds often don't distinguish between behavior and impulse, we can reflexively react to impulses in the same way we react to the behaviors themselves. If hitting is forbidden, we'll tend to relate to the impulse to hit as forbidden.

Usually, engaging in forbidden behavior is tremendously upsetting; even unacceptable. Having forbidden impulses or engaging in forbidden behaviors is sometimes enough negative emotional arousal to block our explicit memory, leaving us learning exclusively with our emotions, body, and behavioral predispositions involved in implicit memory. A common result of this is losing our conscious awareness of forbidden feelings or impulses. This is a form of dissociation. Let's examine some typical taboo feelings and impulses in American society that can result in such dissociation:

- All human cultures have an incest taboo. Sex with a family member, or *the impulse to be sexual with a family member,* is usually forbidden.

- Sexual behavior for children in all situations and for adults in all but a few culturally permitted situations, or *the impulse to engage in such behaviors,* is frequently forbidden.

- Physical violence to self or another, or *the impulse to engage in physical violence,* in response to extreme emotion is usually forbidden.

- Explicit talk about bodily functions, sexual organs or behavior, death or dying, or graphic violence, or *the impulses to engage in such talk,* is frequently forbidden.

If we have feelings or impulses that we dissociate from, we tend to block conscious explicit memory where we are aware something is being remembered. This can leave us at the mercy of the neural networks we developed involving unconscious, implicit memories. We will tend to keep activating the states of consciousness associated with those neural networks (which include emotions, distorted perspectives, and defensive impulses) until we develop enough self-reflective skills to bring this material into conscious awareness where we can process and integrate it into a "larger" self. If unobstructed, our natural developmental rhythm is experience, self-reflection, self-discovery, and integration into more complex and inclusive perspectives and wider ranges of available responses.

Attunement to self is compassionately feeling into self with the intent of serving the highest good. Compassionate awareness of, and integration of, different aspects of self is healthy since it leads to a "larger," more coherent, and inclusive self. Dissociation from different aspects of ourselves blocks development and creates problems for us individually. Since we are interconnected with family members, it is also likely to create problems for them.

The following is a dinner conversation at Harry and Rachel's house a month before Brian was sent away. Four-year-old Hannah is sitting next to Rachel, eight-year-old Albert is sitting across from them, and Harry and Brian are facing each other at the head and foot of the table respectively. A family favorite dinner of roast chicken and vegetables is well under way when Rachel decides to bring up a sensitive subject:

> Rachel: (*"It's better to talk about it when we're all here, and Brian is less likely to walk out."*) "The school called and said that Brian was truant again today." (She looks nervously back and forth between Harry and Brian. Rachel has deliberately waited until the family are half way through dinner in the hopes that a reasonable discussion is more likely when they're eating together, one of the few family rituals that Brian still participates in.)
>
> Brian: "So, what?"
>
> Harry: "So, what? Is that all you have to say? Were you out using drugs with your friends?"

Brian: (Contemptuously.) "It's none of your business what I do."

Harry: "Don't use that tone with me." (He's stopped eating and is glaring at Brian.)

Rachel: (*"I hate it when Harry's like this."*) "I thought we could have a civilized discussion."

Hannah: (She tips over her milk onto her lap, and starts to cry.) "Oh no! Mommy, I made a mess on my dress." (Rachel starts dealing with the crisis.)

Albert: (He quickly eats two more bites and tries to excuse himself.) "Excuse me, I've got homework."

Harry: "Don't you dare leave this table!" (Albert looks down in shame.)

Brian: "He didn't do anything, why do you have to be such a dick?"

Harry: "God damn it, you're grounded! You can't use that kind of language at the table!"

Brian: "What kind of God damn language is that?" (Harry gets up threateningly.)

Rachel: "Stop it! Both of you, stop it! This is horrible. Look what it's doing to Hannah." (Hannah is crying hysterically, and the rest of the family feels ashamed.)

There is a lot of violence occurring in this scene. Brian's "So what?" and contemptuous tones were angry attacks on his parents for calling him on his failures at school. Harry's bullying tone and threatening references were emotional blows at first Brian for being hostile and contemptuous, and then Albert for trying to get away from the ugly scene. Albert's shame at his father's attack and later at Hannah's distress were violent reactions directed at himself. In a family with two powerful, assertive masculine figures like Harry and Brian, Albert has instinctively learned to direct his hostile impulses inward rather than risk being emotionally or physically dominated. Hannah's accident with the milk and her subsequent hysterical tears were violent responses to the tension in the air. Rachel's hostile tone with "civilized discussion" (directed mostly at Harry, whose demeaning style was repulsive to her), her "Stop it!" comments, and her shaming the rest of the family for Hannah's distress all involved varying degrees of violent lashing out.

The problem with the above scene is not that any one component is particularly toxic or irresolvable. This is a fight that is typical of countless negative dramas being played out daily around family dinner tables. You've probably participated in scenes that are just as nasty and uncaring. The problem here is that, in the face of the emerging violence, Rachel and Harry didn't start consciously seeking attunement.

Why pick on Rachel and Harry? There were three other people there: Brian, Albert, and Hannah. Aren't they also responsible for everything they experience and do?

The answer is, in a healthy family there is a hierarchy of authority and responsibility that starts at the top with Mom and Dad.[14] It's great when kids attune in response to defensive states, but the way they learn how to do this is by having parents who feel a sense of responsibility, *when they enter defensive states,* to attune to themselves, their spouse, and their children. Rachel and Harry didn't do this, and so the drama cycled out of control, leaving everyone feeling bad and no one feeling a healthy sense of resolution or triumph.

Let's examine an alternate scenario, with Rachel seeking attunement when she becomes consciously aware of her defensive state:

Brian: "It's none of your business what I do."

Harry: "Don't use that tone with me!"

Rachel: (She feels the violence in the room, and has the impulse to attack Harry. Instead she attunes, *"You're mad, you hate it when Harry goes off, and you want to blast him. That won't help. He's as worried about Brian as you are. Harry probably doesn't even know he's losing it.")* "Harry, I'm mad and feel like arguing. You're mad and are trying to get Brian to be reasonable, and I don't think he can right now. Let's talk to him after dinner."

Harry: (He's still in a defensive state and is feeling unjustly accused.) "You're the one who brought it up."

Rachel: (Again, she feels a flash of anger at Harry and an impulse to throw the potatoes in his face, followed by shame at the impulse. *"Of course you're mad at him. He's the father. He should be using a good tone. Try one more time. If it doesn't work, handle him like we talked about in therapy.")* "I know I brought it up. I'm mad too. It's not working. I think you and I need get organized and then talk to Brian later."

Brian: (He's surrendering to his defensive state.) "It won't make any difference. You can't force me to do what I don't want to do."

Harry: (He feels a blinding flash of rage at this, but Rachel's attunement has evoked a complementary state in him, and he's now struggling to self-regulate. *"She's right. This isn't doing any good. Get hold of yourself. At least you can be soothing to Rachel and the little kids."* He takes a deep breath and speaks as calmly as he can.) "Thanks, Rachel, you're right. I'm sorry, when I get mad I start pushing people around. We'll talk about it later."

Rachel: (At this point she feels intense gratitude to Harry for backing off. She's literally attracted by his maturity; not primarily in the sexual sense, but in the sense that she's now drawn towards him rather than repulsed by him.) "Thanks Harry."

Brian: (Emotionally he's warmed by their mature interaction, but, surrendering to his defensive state, he keeps attacking, trying to get relief by hurting his father.) "You're so pussy-whipped." (Rachel and Harry are attuned to each other at this moment, and they look at each other and start to laugh.)

Harry: "Right son. You're mom just dominates me." (Now Albert laughs, and Hannah, feeling an alleviation of tension, laughs also.)

Brian: (He feels pulled by their love and attunement but resists challenging his distorted perspectives and destructive impulses. In spite of himself, he backs off.) "Whatever."

Here's another alternate scenario with Harry initiating attunement when he becomes aware of his defensive state:

Rachel: "Stop it! Both of you, stop it! This is horrible, look what it's doing to Hannah."

Harry: (He hears her contempt for him, and sees it in her face. He blames Brian and has an brief image of slapping Brian's smirk off his face. He struggles to attune. *"Watch out. He needs help, not you bullying him. You are way too angry to talk to Brian right now. Rachel's really upset and mad at you, but she's right. This is awful for her, and you're not helping."*) "You're right, Rachel, I'm sorry. Here, Hannah, let's go change you into your PJ's. It's almost bedtime."

Hannah: (Sobbing.) "But I haven't taken my bath yet." (This is so cute that everyone exchanges a smile.)

Harry: (He can tell Rachel is less angry with him, and he's now developing a direction of how to help the family.) "Good point, sweetheart. Let's start your bath, and you can have it after dinner. Albert, if you're done, you can go do homework. I'm sorry I used that angry tone with you. You didn't do anything wrong." (Albert immediately feels affectionate connection with Harry and a sense that compassion and justice are being served; indicators that repair is happening from the injuries he was experiencing. He gratefully says "Thank you," and leaves the table.)

Brian: (He's guilty and ashamed now for causing an ugly scene, but is too locked into his angry, distorted state to participate in repair. He attacks himself, unconsciously holding onto his defensive hunger for violence, *"Brian, you're such an asshole."* He sullenly finishes his dinner, resolving to sneak out and smoke pot later with his friends.)

In these last two scenes, Rachel and Harry were aware of their anger and their violent impulses, but accepted them and took on the responsibilities of attuning to themselves and their family. Further, they stopped pathologizing the children for their defensive states and instead tried to help the kids deal with them. Hannah and Albert got acceptance and repair, and Brian got acceptance and boundaries, as his parents handled him as best they could. As a result, the conflict de-escalated, and Rachel and Harry felt closer as a couple. Either Rachel or Harry denying (or dissociating from) their inner experience would have resulted in more repulsion and negative drama, since they would have probably continued to blame each other and Brian for the current problems instead of taking personal responsibility to attune. Later on, after either of the attuned scenarios, Rachel and Harry were more likely to feel intimate and grateful for each other as they discussed the situation; specifically the emerging decision to find a placement for Brian that could address his emotional pain and destructive behaviors.

John Gottman has found that self-reported "happy couples" have positive idealizations of each other. I suspect that he might have slightly misinterpreted his data. I've found that happy couples get progressively better at accessing their most caring sides and evoking the most caring side of their partner. This leads them to identify each other by the best in each of them, rather than being put off and dismayed by their worst aspects. My violent side is no threat to you if I take responsibility for it and don't let you get hurt by it. If I can reach through my anger and violent impulses to try to serve love, I'm most likely to both attract similar behavior in you and to be attractive to you. If you're struggling to hold onto your violent side and try to love me through your defensive states, I'm likely to respond in kind and be attracted and impressed with your efforts. This is one way attuned states evoke complementary positive reactions in our partners.

Violence and sex.

If you are a feminine person, you have likely had the fantasy or experience of being ravished. This means that a powerful, trustable masculine partner has felt into you, discerned that you want to be swept up and forced to surrender emotionally and erotically, and has confidently engaged in that behavior, evoking passion, surrender, and devotional love on your part.

If you are a masculine person, you have likely had the fantasy or experience of ravishing your partner. This means that you have felt into her heart, perceived her feminine radiance, hungered to possess her erotically, and, staying connected to her pleasure, have taken charge of her body and aggressively opened her to progressively deeper erotic bliss.

The above descriptions reflect two of the most common sexual fantasies my clients have reported over the years. These are the feminine ravishment fantasy that can be found in most romance novels and the masculine fantasy of aggressively opening an eager lover to deeper and deeper bliss that she expresses through movement, sound, and breath. Both of these experiences require us to embrace our violent side. As David Deida maintains in his lectures and books, the difference between rape and ravishment is love.[15] If I can attune and love you through my anger, that anger becomes an energy source for my love and can add fuel to love's fire. As a masculine partner, the archetype for this is divine ravishment. As a feminine partner, the archetype is erotic surrender expressed through pleasure in the body. We will deal more extensively with these erotic polarities in Chapter Eight, Erotic Attunement.

1. Porges (2006)

2. Johnson (2005)

3. Ogden (2006)

4. Wilber (2000)

5. Porges (2006)

6. Lemonick (2005)

7. Bandura (1973)

8. *Ibid*

9. Lemonick (2005)

10. Wilber (2000)

11. Siegal (2005)

12. Witt (2005)

13. Cassidy, J., and Shaver, P. (Eds.). (1999)

14. Minuchin (1974)

15. Deida (2004)

8

Erotic Attunement

Here are Rachel and Harry six months after they met. Both in their mid twenties, they just got home from kayaking out in the surf on a bright winter day. Exhilarated from the ocean, covered in salt, Harry makes it into the shower first. Rachel joins him, and the sight of her naked body instantly turns him on. He embraces her under the warm shower. His relaxed masculinity, especially after he has been authoritatively showing her how to maneuver a kayak in surf, is magnetically attractive to her, and she surrenders into his arms, moaning in pleasure. They make urgent love in the shower and start laughing at the end when they run out of hot water just as Harry is having an orgasm.

Here are Rachel and Harry eighteen years later, the night of the dinner argument about Brian's truancy. The argument didn't end well. Brian stormed out of the house with Harry shouting at him and decided to stay with his friend, David. Rachel had to spend extra time soothing the two younger children, who remained distressed until they finally went to sleep. Rachel and Harry remained mostly silent as they got ready for bed. Harry feels angry and ashamed, and Rachel angry and hopeless:

Harry: "All right. I'm sorry, I shouldn't have yelled. I just don't know what to do."

Rachel: (She's heard his apologies before. He's often contrite after losing his temper, but he seems to keep on losing it in the same way. Nevertheless, she can feel his sincerity, and she loves him.) "It wasn't you getting mad. It was how you ignored me when I said we needed to calm down. We talked about it in therapy."

Harry: "I can't stand it when Brian treats you disrespectfully."

Rachel: "It's not my favorite thing either. Hannah asked if you were going to hit Brian."

Harry: (Insulted and genuinely confused.) "I've never hit the kids. Where did she get that idea?"

Rachel: "You don't know how scary you are when you yell."

Harry: (He feels a curious little rush of power that he's scary, followed by shame that his four-year-old would even imagine he'd strike one of the kids. He reaches across the bed and puts his arm around her. She feels him loving her and, attracted to him in this state, snuggles up next to him and lets out a deep breath. Harry is moved to reassure her.) "It will be OK, Rachel. We've really only just started therapy. Brian's basically good. We'll figure something out."

Rachel: (She relaxes into her body for the first time this evening, stretches luxuriantly, and hugs him.) "All I know is I love all of you."

Harry: (Suddenly attracted, he pulls her a little closer, which she instinctively responds to by snuggling into his chest. He lets his right hand glide down to her hip, and kisses her on the head.)

Rachel: (She gets the message he wants sex and instantly feels resistant. Too many times, after fights, Harry has wanted to have sex to make things right. She stiffens and recoils slightly, not wanting to start another fight.) "Not tonight, Harry, I'm too tired and burned out." (As she says the words, she feels the weight of her fatigue and concern come down over her, and she is suddenly exhausted.)

Harry: (Feeling rejected, angry, and somehow ashamed that he's done something wrong, he turns abruptly away from her.) "Sure, whatever you say."

A lot has happened in the past eighteen years. Rachel and Harry are older, more experienced, burdened by many more responsibilities, and are in the process of raising three children, one of whom is regularly out of control. These factors heavily influence their relationship as lovers, but not as much as the stories they tell themselves about their lives. These personal narratives are how Harry and Rachel organize and understand the past, develop expectations for the future, and inform their decisions in the present moment.

Harry tells himself the story that sex is something Rachel gives and he takes and that, if the choice is entirely up to her, she would usually just as soon not take the trouble. He has guilty masturbation fantasies about hot babes who love sex, but assumes that hot babes don't really exist except in the first years of a relationship, in illicit sex (like affairs), or in "good" marriages that some people (but nobody he knows) have.

Rachel tells herself the story that Harry will never truly understand her need for intimacy and romance, that all he's interested in is for her to help him have some kind of orgasm, and that she's no longer that attractive because she's put on twenty pounds and aged eighteen years. Both assume that the natural order of things is for couples to be passionate in the beginning and then fade into partners who can, once in a while, mildly enjoy each other erotically.

There is a lot of truth to these narratives. Age, fatigue, responsibility, stress, unresolved conflict, and decreased self-esteem (not to mention nursing and sleep deprivation) all tend to depress libido and interfere with erotic polarity.

Most relationships begin with a love affair that involves increased brain levels of dopamine and norephrenephrine, excitement neurotransmitters.[1] Romantic infatuation, which can last from a few days to several years, is a biochemical joy-ride that enhances sexual polarity and gives people a free pass from many of their relational defensive patterns. Under the influence of romantic infatuation it is easy to imagine effortless hot sex continuing indefinitely and relationship problems automatically solved by two passionate partners who can't get enough of each other. It often feels like a rude awakening as romantic infatuation fades and couples enter the bonding stage of relationship.

As couples become more intimate, they begin to recapitulate the levels of closeness and connection with each other that they had growing up with parents and siblings. This stage involves increased brain levels of oxytocin, a bonding neurotransmitter.[2] As partners "feel" more like family members, relational defensive systems that we developed in our families of origin can arise when cued by perceived threat (like loss of romantic infatuation). These defensive systems are embedded in our implicit memory, where we can have powerful associations and habitual responses with no sense that something is being remembered. When we feel threatened we can find ourselves attacking, defending, accusing, and assuming in ways that are eerily similar to how our original family members related when stressed.

When Harry was a child, he frequently fought with his older brother, Dustin, who hated it when Harry was born and parental attention was no longer exclusively focused on him. Their father was frequently gone, and their mother, though often loving and affectionate, solved many distressing conflicts by raging and bullying both boys. When threatened, Harry's nervous system was programmed to fight and dominate, but then to crave feminine soothing. When he felt threatened by Rachel he would naturally try to protect himself by swelling up with anger. Later, feeling wounded and lonely, he hungered for reassuring feminine caress and love, leading him to make sexual overtures. This dynamic is often present in "make-up sex."

Rachel had a younger sister and brother that she felt parental and protective towards. Both her mom and dad were successful lawyers who were frequently busy with work. Rachel took on many parental responsibilities at a young age, and learned that her comfort, pleasure, and fulfillment were secondary to her busy parents and needy siblings. Even though she complied with these "unfair" family rules, and instinctively concealed her own yearnings and resentments, she secretly told herself stories of how selfish everyone else was when her feelings and needs were ignored. When Harry behaved badly, she was easily moved to contempt, denial of her own needs and bodily sensations, and impulses to accommodate, or withdraw and disconnect for relief.

People's narratives are not set in stone. We can change our stories to reflect deeper, more compassionate understanding of the past, more hopeful and positive expectations for the future, and clearer directions about what creates the most health and love in the present moment. Such reorganization of narrative requires self-reflection and maturation but is also enormously helped by understanding the dynamics of polarity and erotic attunement.

Erotic polarity

As I explained to Jim and Sally in Chapter Two, everyone has both a feminine and masculine aspect, but, in our deepest heart, we usually have a more feminine or masculine essence. This is especially true in our erotic relationships, since, at any given moment, erotic charge between two people is largely a function of how completely they are occupying the masculine and feminine poles of erotic polarity. David Deida maintains that the more a masculine person surrenders the feminine to his partner, and the more a feminine person surrenders the masculine to her partner, the greater intensity of erotic polarity.[3]

There are powerful evolutionary forces that mandate this process. In hunter-gatherer societies, women with the most erotic radiance and capacity for caring and affiliation would be most attractive to a man, and most likely to help him pass on his genes. This is because he would want to sexually possess her feminine form, and she would be most likely to care for and protect his children in the company of other women. Similarly, a man who was trustable, unrecoiling, resolute, committed to his mission, and deeply interested in knowing, claiming and possessing her would be likely to attract a woman because his social status, strength, protection, and interest in (and knowledge of) her would help her and her children survive and thrive. Feminine erotic radiance and warmth attract masculine presence and claim, which, in turn, attract feminine radiance and warmth, and so on. This is part of the dance of erotic polarity.

Human consciousness has added spiritual wild cards to this evolutionary process. Humans can, through conscious intent, increasingly direct their own development as they mature. Since our nervous systems help guide the growth of our children's nervous systems, and evoke complementary states in our intimates' nervous systems, we also influence the course of each other's personal evolution.

What are the states of consciousness where you feel the most sexy, attractive, and attracted to your spouse? What are your spouse's states of consciousness that are most attractive and sexy to you? What can you do to evoke and practice these states in yourself and support them in your spouse? Erotically attuned couples develop in these areas, consciously cultivating personal and relational integration over the years to create more consistent and powerful love and passion.

If Rachel and Harry knew these principles and practices, the above exchange might have gone like this:

> Harry: (His right hand glides down to her hip and he kisses her on the head. He desires her erotically, but understands that he has earlier surrendered to his bullying defense and that it makes him less trustable to Rachel.) "I know I need to work on not blowing up. I know it hurts you and the kids. I'm working on it, and I'll get better at it."

> Rachel: (She relaxes in response to Harry knowing her enough to be aware of her concerns. She feels the sexual overture, and has reflexive resistance, but attunes to herself and recognizes that this is her old pattern of angrily resisting giving someone the love they want after they've hurt her. She breathes deeply and relaxes into her body, reminding herself that Harry is working on loving her and the kids better, and that loving connection would be fun and healing right now. She focuses on feeling the pleasure of his warmth, love, and touch, and moans softly, pulling his head towards her for a deep kiss. They make love and feel progressively more connected and attuned.)

Similarly, if Rachel were truly exhausted from the stressful evening, but both were attuned, it might have gone like this:

> Rachel: (She feels the sexual overture, but knows she is too tired and sore emotionally to relax into lovemaking.) "I love you, but I'm just too burned out right now to make love. Maybe tomorrow morning, if we can wake up before the kids."

Harry: (He's disappointed and has a flash of shame and then rage at her "rejection." He recognizes this as an old pattern of not trusting Rachel to be loving and sexual. He self-soothes and directs himself to be a present, trustable man. *"She had a horrible night, and she's been working hard at opening and loving you erotically. She never used to say things like, 'Let's do it tomorrow.' Make it safe for her to say 'no.' Surprise her by being excellent."* He pulls her closer.) "I understand, honey. You were great tonight, and you're still the sexiest woman on the block. I'll try to find a time tomorrow to make an offer you can't refuse."

Rachel: (She smiles at his *Godfather* reference, and thinks to herself, *"He never used to be understanding when I said 'no.'"*) "You're nice." (Feeling safe and loved, she cuddles up next to him and goes to sleep, while he holds her and feels tender, strong, and protective.)

Because of sexual inhibitions and taboos, most of us are vulnerable in our sexuality and reluctant to share many sexual interests, needs, resentments, and yearnings. An erotically attuned couple realizes this, and *each feels a sense of responsibility* to support his or her own sexuality and help their spouse feel attractive and fulfilled erotically.

To do this, we have to offer our partner authentic gifts. If Rachel grits her teeth and offers Harry some kind of sexual experience while withholding her own pleasure, she's teaching herself to despise Harry, and Harry to not trust her "yes." If Harry takes "no" for an answer and tells himself a story about how he is unable to attract Rachel, or how Rachel is unable to erotically surrender, he's teaching himself to resent Rachel and to feel powerless erotically. Similarly, if she's complying without pleasure and he doesn't perceive and respond in a loving way, she will experience his lack of sensitivity as collapse, and they will be practicing sex without positive emotional connection; another recipe for resentment and distrust.

Erotic attunement involves imagining what it's like in your partner's mind and body as you relate verbally, emotionally, and physically. Many times over the years, I've talked to men and women who believed that their spouse had no idea, or did not really care about their experience. "I've told my husband lots of times that he's too rough when he handles my breasts." "My wife would just as soon get it over with. She thinks if I come that I've had a great time." "He has no idea what turns me on." "She has to always have it exactly the same way." These couples suffer from lack of attunement. If I'm not feeling into and accepting myself, I'm not going to give you clear signals about what is more or less pleasurable or connected. If I'm not feeling into and accepting you, I'm unlikely to notice when you give me signals about how connected or turned on you are. Such processes have consequences that reach far beyond the bedroom. Feeling "felt" by our spouse and arranging for our spouse to feel "felt" by us are central aspects of most successful marriages.

In the dance of erotic engagement, the masculine is the leader and the feminine is the follower. He offers her direction as to what serves the highest good and then resolutely accepts, with good humor, whatever she decides. She feels into him and, if he's trustable, shows him her pleasure through her body with breath, movement, and sound, and if he's not, reveals her suffering through breath, movement, and sound. If his feminine partner recoils, the masculine adjusts towards presence, connection, and humor until she lets him know with her pleasure that he is trustable again.

Men and women can occupy either pole of erotic polarity in general, and on any given occasion. Accomplished lovers learn to automatically trade positions (both literally and figuratively) during lovemaking to sustain and enhance polarity, depending upon their natural tendencies and the rhythms and demands of the moment. In most erotic relationships, one partner will more naturally occupy the masculine pole and the other the feminine pole.

Relationships are complex. Most people can have more feminine and more masculine moments. Rachel, an accountant, did the books for the family, and Harry deferred to her financial direction in this area. Harry occasionally got up when Hannah had a nightmare, and held and comforted her without demand (a central aspect of feminine healing) until she went to back to sleep. Erotic attunement involves knowing your own masculine/feminine aspects and deepest sexual essence and consciously coordinating these forces with your partner to create the most love in your marriage and family.

How we can use erotic attunement to be better parents.

Our children are born sensually relating to the world and developing as sexual beings. Boys and girls develop differently physically, neurologically, morally, interpersonally, and psychosexually. Some children are aware of themselves as sexual beings as toddlers, and some first encounter identifiable sexual feelings in adolescence. Some children experiment sexually with looking/touching games with other children, and some children are completely private with their sexuality until they start having boyfriends or girlfriends. Some children feel sexual charges with exclusively opposite sex partners, some with exclusively same sex partners, and some with masculine and feminine partners. All of the above can be part of normal, healthy development.[4]

Parents can feel their children's emergent sexuality and be attracted, repulsed, neutral, or confused. These reactions also can be part of normal, healthy development.

What supports optimal psychosexual development in our children?

First of all, I want to compliment you for reading this far and considering these issues. To be able to do this, you are successfully resisting cultural prohibitions around acknowledging your children's sexual nature, and considering your own energetic interface with your children's sexuality. The following is an exchange that's typical of many I've had over the years. This is a session with a thirty-five-year-old woman named Betsy, who came in to work on relationship problems:

Keith: (Knowing that our patterns for relating are partly programmed by implicit, unconscious learning throughout our development, I frequently ask clients how affection was communicated when they were children.) "How was love expressed in your family?"

Betsy: "Our parents told us they loved us, and they kissed us good-night. You know, the usual. My mom was the more touchy-feely one."

Keith: "How do you mean?"

Betsy: "Dad just seemed to stop being affectionate when we were kids."

Keith: "He stopped being affectionate in what ways?"

Betsy: "When I was a little girl, I used to climb into his lap. When I was about seven, he wouldn't let me anymore. I never knew why."

Keith: "Why do you think?"

Betsy: "He said I was too big. But Mom got in his lap, and my younger brother was as big as me. I figured he just didn't like me as much any more."

Keith: "That doesn't make sense with what you've told me about your Dad. You've described him as having always been dedicated to you, your brother, and your mother."

Betsy: "Maybe it was because I was a girl."

Keith: "What do you mean?"

Betsy: "The older I got, the more he made critical comments about my clothes being too revealing, and me not being careful enough around boys. It wasn't fair. My boyfriends were good guys, and my family seemed to like them."

Keith: "Maybe he was a little scared of your developing sexuality."

Betsy: "He never said anything positive about me and sexuality; that's for sure."

I wouldn't know unless I spoke frankly with Betsy's dad, and even then he might not be conscious of, or remember, what made him stop cuddling his seven-year-old daughter, but I suspect he had some experience of feeling erotic energy with seven-year-old Betsy, and was so alarmed by it that he physically withdrew from her. Since we're not supposed to feel sexual energy with our children, if we do we're likely to experience shame, guilt, and alarm. Some fathers, in response to such experiences, stop touching their children altogether, leaving a hurt and confused child wondering what happened.

The impulse is not the act and yet, if we are not aware of how normal development works and are not attuned to our own feelings, thoughts, and impulses, we can react to the pleasure of cuddling our children with alarm. Pleasurable touch is an important part of development. Infants will actually die if not touched regularly by a caregiver, and monkeys raised in the absence of parental touch were relationally and emotionally crippled.[5]

Feeling into and accepting ourselves, while feeling into and accepting our children, will sometimes lead to encountering erotic polarities. Erotic *touch* is traumatic between parents and children, between older children and younger children, and sometimes even between same age children.

However, erotic *feelings, and impulses* occur normally in various forms in most families. It's quite possible that when adorable seven-year-old Betsy climbed into her father's lap, he felt some tingle of erotic polarity and, alarmed and ashamed, decided to "protect her" by not touching her anymore except in very circumscribed ways such as goodnight kisses, or awkward hello and goodbye hugs. Worse, his sense of alarm could have been communicated to her in the form of her sensing her sexuality was wrong and distressing to her father. Since we tend to parent ourselves (and others) the way we've been parented, this could lead to Betsy feeling ashamed of her sexuality and being profoundly reluctant to explicitly discuss personal sexual issues. Incorporating these defenses into her marriage and parenting style, Betsy is at risk to pathologize erotic feelings, impulses, and explicit talk with her husband and children, thus endangering erotic polarity with her husband, and giving her children the message to not feel or discuss sexuality, and so on through the generations.

We feel energetic polarities constantly throughout each day. When I look at the ocean and feel pleasure, there is an energetic polarity between me and the ocean. The same can happen with a flower, a mountain, a beautiful car, my tennis opponent, a baby, or a feminine person. The more I am aware of these energetic polarities, the more I can adjust them to serve the highest good. Some of these polarities have a sexual component, and some do not. This is simply the physics of relationships, and is innocent. If I surrender to impulses to *critically judge* myself or others for my reactions, I create unnecessary suffering. Sexuality has been pathologized, and women have been attacked and blamed for their sexuality for thousands of years in almost every agrarian society that has arisen throughout human history. Today, in some countries, women must completely conceal their forms so as not to "tempt" men. Pathologizing sexuality and the feminine can interfere with both men and women's interpersonal and psychosexual development.

Attunement is feeling into myself and another with caring intent.

If a parent feels sexual polarity with a child, the highest good is served by the child being protected from *sexual contact* with a parent, while still feeling loved and supported in *their own emergent sexuality*. Consider the following dialog between Betsy's husband, Kurt, and Imogene, their twelve-year-old daughter:

> Imogene: (She walks into the living room in a pair of super short pink hot pants and a tiny halter top that emphasizes her budding breasts. She's also wearing makeup, earrings, and pink nail polish.) "I'm going to the mall with Candi."

> Kurt: (His first association when he sees his daughter is the teen-aged hooker played by Jodie Foster in *Taxi Driver*. He knows that middle school girls often compete to see who can wear the most provocative outfits, but this one is clearly over the top. He feels a distressing sexual tingle, but realizes this is a natural reaction to the image his daughter has just constructed.) "I'm sorry, you can't wear that outfit. It's way too sexy."

> Imogene: "Why not? Lots of girls wear outfits like this."

Kurt: "When you get older and have a lover, you should wear that outfit for him. He'll love it. Meanwhile, it's too sexy for a twelve-year-old. The message is, 'Give me lots of sexual attention.'"

Imogene: "That's gross. I just think it's cute."

Kurt: (He's more comfortable now. He's adjusted his own erotic polarity and is amused by Imogene's denial of her obvious attempt to appear as a sexually mature young woman.) "I think it's great that you want to experiment with different looks. You're growing into a beautiful young woman. It's fine with me if you wear skimpy outfits at home or playing dress up with your friends. You are not experienced enough with men to wear that kind of outfit in public. It will pull erotic attention, and, if the guy is immature or loaded, it might be scary attention."

Imogene: "I don't play dress up! I'm not a little girl any more."

Kurt: "Sorry, wrong words. The bottom line, lose the make up and put on another outfit." (Imogene sulks off to change.)

Kurt felt his own sexual reaction to Imogene's erotic outfit, normalized it, attuned to her need for instruction and boundaries, and provided them. Imogene was not allowed to be inappropriately provocative, but her sexuality was honored and even appreciated by her father. This is a father using erotic attunement to support his daughter's development.

Another example of a parent using erotic attunement to support their child's development is the following exchange between Sally and her five-year-old son Jake. She has just walked into his room, and he and his friend Sara are naked on the bed, giggling and touching each other. Jake has an erection:

Sally: (Shocked, she feels a rush of embarrassment, accompanied by anger at Jake. *Take a deep breath and get hold of yourself. They are just little kids playing sexual games.*) "What are you two up to? You might want to get dressed." (The children quickly pull on some clothes.)

Jake: (He knows he's breaking some kind of rule with Sara and feels ashamed and guilty.) "Nothing."

Sara: (This is especially humiliating for her since Sally is not her mom. She looks down.) "I'm sorry."

Sally: (She has an image of Sara's mother, Allison, a devout Christian who's unlikely to be supportive of sex games. *Sara's parents are going to freak out over this. Support the children; they look guilty, and they were just exploring. Let them know they're fine, and that sexuality is OK.")* "It looks like you two are playing looking/touching games." (They both nod.) "Sara, is it OK with your Mom that you and Jake play looking/touching games?"

Sara: "I don't know."

Sally: "That's all right. We'll just ask her when she picks you up. Were you guys having fun?"

Jake: "Yes, Mom. I was showing Sara my penis. She has a 'gina."

Sally: "You mean, a vagina?" (Both children nod.) "Boys have penises and girls have vaginas. When boys feel turned on, their penis get stiff like Jake's was. That's called an 'erection.' Girls have little clitorises at the top of their vagina. When girls get turned on, their clitoris gets a little bigger, and it feels good to be touched, but it doesn't get as big as an erection. Well, lets put on your clothes and go get lunch. We need to ask Sara's mom about what rules she has about looking/touching games."

Sally felt her own sexual embarrassment, and also resentment at Jake for creating a difficult situation with Sara's family. She also empathetically perceived the kids' guilt and embarrassment, as well as the pleasure and titillation of their sexual game. Tolerating her discomfort, she tried to support their self-esteem and development, normalize their game, give them important sexual information, and direct them skillfully into another activity.

She also asked if they were having fun. This is a question that is rarely explored with children and teens when discussing sexual activity. Was it fun? The purpose of sexual play at all ages is intimacy and pleasure. The way we teach this is by including the important pleasure dimension in sexual processing. If the kids were older, Sally might have distinguished between sensual and erotic pleasure. Sensual pleasure is enjoying bodily sensation, and does not necessarily involve sexual arousal. Erotic pleasure involves a pleasurable sexual component, usually accompanied by warmth and tingling in the genitals and pelvic area.

Later, while the kids were playing in the back yard, Sally has the following conversation with Allison, who's come to pick up Sara. First Sally tries relating, but, when this results in Allison accelerating into a defensive state, she shifts into handling:

Sally: (Her whole body feels resistant to talking explicitly about sexual matters, especially involving children, but she knows it's the caring thing to do.

She takes a deep breath. *"Just spit it out. If you don't mention it, Sara might, and then who knows what she'll say?")* "I walked into Jake's room, and the kids were naked, and Jake had an erection."

Allison: (She's stunned. In her world, five-year-old kids don't get naked together, and it feels horrible that her daughter saw an erection.) "You mean, he was molesting her?"

Sally: (*"Damn!. I knew it. Just calm down. She needs help with this."*) "I don't think two five-year-olds playing a looking/touching game is a molest. They said they were having fun, but I told them to put on their clothes and come have lunch, and that you and I would talk about it when you came to pick Sara up."

Allison: (Her emotional window of tolerance has been exceeded by this, and she unconsciously is going through the shame, rage cycle.) "Sara can't come here anymore. What were you thinking, leaving them alone in the bedroom?"

Sally: (*"Handle her. She can't tolerate direct conversation about this."*) "I'm sorry I left them alone in the room. I won't do it again, and I'll tell Jake he can't play looking/touching games with Sara. It would be a shame if the kids lost each other as friends because of this."

Allison: "What's wrong with him? Where did he learn this stuff?"

Sally: (Now she's angry. The implication that Jake is sick in some way for being sexually curious arouses her protective instinct. *"How dare you accuse my son? Come on, Sally, calm down. Try to help her and help the kids."*) "Well, I think it's just normal curiosity, but I know this great therapist, Mary West, and I'll take Jake in for a session, just to be sure there's no problem. I'll give you her number. If you're worried, you can go in with Sara and talk about it. She's an expert with children, and I think she's wonderful." (Sally writes out the name and number on a Post-it, and hands it to Allison.)

Allison: (Sally's soothing tones, and practical suggestions are calming her down. As she begins to enter a state of healthy response, her basic, caring nature reasserts itself.) "Thank you. I'll have to talk to Paul, but this sounds reasonable."

Sally: (*"Tell her what you told the children."*) "I explained to the kids about how a penis gets stiff when a boy gets turned on, and how girls have a clitoris. I didn't want Sara to feel one down because she can't have an erection.

I'm sorry if I broke any of your family rules, but I thought the kids needed a little sex education to understand what they were experiencing."

Allison: (Uncomfortable with these explicit sexual references, she is soothed by Sally's calm tone and obvious dedication to the children.) "I guess that's OK. God knows what I would have done."

Sally: "It was a shock, I'll tell you. But they were really cute and innocent." (Both mothers smile.)

This was a difficult situation for Sally and Allison. Sally had to manage her own inhibitions and distress, feel into the children's experience, feel into Allison's experience, and try to serve everybody. Allison was shocked, caught up in a defensive state that she had no conscious awareness of, and then forced to deal explicitly with forbidden material. Luckily, Sally's attunement provided a path through this sexual/emotional minefield.

That night at Allison's house, things go a little differently. Sixteen-year-old daughter Clair is sitting next to Sara, who's across the table from Paul and Allison, and the family has just started dinner. Paul owns a body shop in town, and Clair is about to enter her senior year at Santa Barbara High School. Clair has a new boyfriend, Kenny, and she wants to spend the weekend with him and his parents camping at Lake Nacimiento:

Paul: "No way."

Clair: "Come on, Dad. His parents will be there."

Paul: "They're just a couple of old hippies. They let their kids do anything."

Clair: "Kenny's an 'A' student, and you said you like him."

Paul: "I used to go to the lake when I was a teenager, and all I thought about was partying."

Clair: "I wish you'd trust me. I'm not going to be using drugs, and ripping off my clothes and running wild you know."

Allison: "Clair, your sister's at the table."

Allison: "What did I say? You are so overprotective."

Sara: "I showed Jake my 'gina today." (This is met with dead silence.)

Paul: "What? Allison?" (Allison gives an abbreviated version of what happened.)

Clair: "That's no big deal. I think Rachel handled it really well."

Paul: "Nobody asked you. I don't like it. What was Rachel thinking letting them be alone together?"

Sara: (She senses the palpable tension that is building, and feels ashamed.) "I'm sorry."

Allison: "You didn't do anything wrong, honey. We're just talking about it."

Clair: "You guys are so uptight about sex."

Paul: "Watch your mouth!"

Clair: "You see? Lighten up."

Paul: "You're grounded, and forget about the lake." (Now Clair tears up.)

Allison: "Rachel gave me the name of a good therapist, maybe we should go."

Clair: "I'm not crazy, though I can't vouch for you and Dad."

Paul: (He's almost exceeded his window of tolerance.) "That's it. Clair, you ..."

Allison: "No. We're all upset. I was upset when I talked to Rachel, but then I felt better. I'm going to make an appointment, and we're going to finish dinner. No more arguing." (The dinner ends in stiff silence.)

Three weeks later they are near the end of their second family session with Mary West, the therapist Rachel recommended to Allison. The Jake and Sara episode was easily dealt with. Mary interviewed Sara, talked to Rachel, and reassured Paul and Allison that everything was fine. Mary suggested that Sara stay with a babysitter, and that Paul, Allison, and Clair come to this meeting, since she knew that the parents would freeze up if certain topics were brought up in front of five-year-old Sara. This second session is digging more deeply into family taboos:

Mary: "It seems against the rules to talk about sex in this family."

Clair: "You can say that again."

Mary: "What about you, Clair? Can you talk to your friends about sex?"

Clair: (Even though she has had relatively few explicit conversations with friends, by contrast to her family they seem wide open.) "Sure." (Paul looks nervous.)

Mary: (*"The poor guy. Living with three females and having to deal with all this uncomfortable material. God knows what his sexual training was."*) "What's going on Paul? You look like you're in pain." (This elicits nervous giggles from Clair and Allison.)

Paul: "I just don't think it's right to talk about this stuff. Why should we? It's simple. We're Christians. You don't have sex until you're married, and that's it."

Mary: (*"Help him understand that he's refining his morals rather than changing them."*) "I agree it's important to have strong moral values in a family, but is it immoral to talk to your girls about their bodies and sexuality? How are they going to find out what sex is, and how to do it? It's not that easy to have a great sex life if you know nothing about it."

Paul: "Allison takes care of that stuff." (Allison looks away. She knows she avoids the subject.)

Clair: "Come on, Dad. Mom has just as much trouble as you. She never lets me do anything, and I'm sixteen. My friends' parents let them stay out till one, and Emily has her own car. Times have changed."

Paul: (He remembers his teenage years of binge drinking and drugging, and having sex with whomever he ended up with at the end of the night, and he feels ashamed and frightened for his daughters. *"Guys just want to get loaded and get laid."*) "You are still so young, and you know what boys want."

Mary: "How was it for you, Paul, when you were a teenager?"

Paul: (Now completely embarrassed, he becomes overwhelmed.) "I can't talk about it. I just want my girls to be safe."

Mary: "Next session I suggest just you and Allison come in. Meanwhile, Clair, do you think you could tell your mother privately what you think is an appropriate level of sexual contact for a sixteen-year-old like you?"

Paul: (Now he's angry.) "What do you mean? There's no appropriate level of premarital sex."

Mary: "How about kissing and hugging? If Clair has a boyfriend, do you think it's appropriate for them to kiss and hug?"

Paul: (*"She's right. A sixteen-year-old should be able to kiss her boyfriend. But not Clair."* He feels confused.) "I just don't want to talk about it."

Allison: "We can have the conversation. I'm actually curious." (Now Clair looks uncomfortable.)

Mary: "You can have the conversation in my office if you'd like."

Clair: (Much to the surprise of Paul and Allison, she immediately agrees.) "That would be much better."

Allison and Paul's family is healthy, successful, and mutually supportive. They mostly share the same solid values. Like many American families, they just happen to be inhibited around sexual issues. Mary has taken all this in and knows that they don't need new values as much as they need to refine old values. Since Paul and Allison are committed to their daughters' happiness and development, she knows they'll eventually be glad to find ways of supporting healthy sexual and interpersonal growth. To do this they need to attune to themselves and each other to differentiate and integrate the parts of themselves that have kept sexual material forbidden to discuss, and have maintained unrealistic and dual standards for sexual behavior. Paul would have less difficulty with a son who was getting more serious with a girlfriend and, instead of stressing abstinence, would be advocating safe sex. He doesn't consciously know this because he's never considered or discussed it with someone he trusts.

Over the next ten sessions, Mary opens them up and teaches them masculine/feminine principles and practices. She helps them refine their standards of caring for self and others and engaging in healthy, responsible behavior *including sexual behavior*. This process, though uncomfortable at times, leaves them a stronger, more attuned family.

1. Fisher (2004)
2. *Ibid*
3. Deida (2004)
4. Levine (2002)
5. Blum (2002)

9

Inclusive and Exclusive Boundaries

We are each a community of many selves, many states, and many capacities.[1] Look inward, and you will discover a tender self, an angry self, a generous self, and a stingy self. We all have a self that needs solitude and a self that needs contact. We have defensive structures and states that resist insight and change, and integrative forces that strive for growth, superior perspectives, and wisdom. We all have a masculine aspect, a feminine aspect, and a deepest sexual essence that is more masculine or more feminine. We frequently change our state in response to who we're with, where we are, and what we're doing.

Most of us function as integrated wholes with an "I" at the center who has always felt the same from our earliest consciousness to the present moment.[2] But that person actually exists within a potentially infinite series of interior relationships that include a complex potpourri of environmental cues, previous associations, implicit and explicit memories, anticipations about the future, and conscious intent. Sometimes all these forces are not cooperatively integrated and aligned. That's when we need boundaries.

Attuning to ourselves and mutually attuning with others involves experiencing a variety of emotions, thoughts, impulses, and perceptions and then, thorough inclusive and exclusive boundaries, directing ourselves toward the perspectives and behaviors that we've concluded are optimal.

Inclusive and exclusive boundaries with ourselves.

Inclusive boundaries with ourselves are those things we insist on including in our individual lives. Brushing my teeth after meals, making my bed each morning, and exercising regularly are all examples of inclusive boundaries with myself.

Exclusive boundaries with ourselves are those things we insist on not including in our individual lives. Examples might be refusing to eat a second piece of cake, drink a third glass of wine, or drive more than ten miles over the speed limit.

Inclusive and exclusive boundaries with others.

Inclusive boundaries with others are those things we insist that others do. Making sure my children say "please" and "thank you," insisting that you're ready to leave in time to catch our plane, and instituting a rule that the kids' homework is done before the TV gets turned on are all examples of inclusive boundaries for others.

Exclusive boundaries with others are those things we insist that others not do, without some form of protest or consequence on our part. "You can't swear at the dinner table," firing an employee who steals, or grounding a teenager for lying are all examples (swearing, stealing, and lying) of behaviors we will not tolerate without action.

Boundaries are attunement in action.

Being an effective parent and a satisfied lover requires regular inclusive and exclusive boundaries. Attunement guides us in discerning our best estimate of what serves everybody. Boundaries are major means of implementing these discernments.

Consider the following exchange between Rachel and Brian, five months after he returned from Mountain View:

Brian: "I want to go out with my friends tonight."

Rachel: (She feels a surge of fear. It was Brian's oppositional teen culture that seemed to consume him before he was sent away. Her impulse is to immediately refuse, but she sets a boundary for herself. *"Don't jump to conclusions. We're supposed to engage in adult dialog if it's possible. Ask him for details."*) "Which friends, going where, and coming home when?"

Brian: "It's Friday night. David and I were just going to hang out and see what's happening."

Rachel: (David was one of Brian's main drug buddies, and she's learned that unstructured time on Friday night is dangerous. She initially tries setting a boundary by relating.) "Sorry. We both know David still smokes pot, and it's too soon for you to be out cruising on Friday night."

Brian: (He has changed significantly since being institutionalized. He has stayed drug free and is motivated to be successful and do right. On the other hand, at almost seventeen he still has an adolescent sense of invulnerability towards many of the world's dangers.) "Come on, Mom. David doesn't smoke around me, and you've got to let me go out sometime."

Rachel: (She wants Brian to have a social life, and she does like David as a person. He's a straight A student and a star on the school tennis team. However, her instincts tell her that unstructured Friday night social time is dangerous.) "David can come over here, but you guys can't go out."

Brian: (His old defensive combativeness is stimulated. Even though he's had eighteen months of intense training to integrate his defensive neural networks into larger, more mature systems that reach for healthy alternatives to transgressive impulses, his defensive reactions will never fully disappear. Under the right conditions, the old amplified or numbed emotions, distorted perspectives, and destructive impulses can show up, and he either successfully attunes through them or not. Right now he's locked into a familiar power struggle.) "There's nothing to do over here. Let me go to his house. You can't keep me locked up."

Rachel: (Her instinct is to say "yes" to her children, but she's learned that's not always in their best interests. *"His counselor told me to never say 'yes' when I feel pressured."*) "I'm sorry, Brian, the answer is 'no.' You need to accept it."

Brian: (Mad now, he becomes reckless.) "That's such bullshit."

Rachel: (Realizing she can't relate cooperatively at this time, she resolves to handle him. *"I've got to set a boundary when he swears at me."*) "You're grounded from the computer tonight for swearing at me. I'm going to stop talking now, before I have to take something else away. After you cool down, I think you're going to want to apologize." (She walks off, shaking.)

Brian: (Muttering to himself, he stalks to his room and throws himself on the bed. *"Screw her. I need to be free. I should just run away."* He hears himself, and finally begins to attune. *"Listen to you. You got pissed off and swore at her, you didn't take 'no' for an answer, and you know you and David like to push the edge. You should apologize."* He feels guilty for backsliding, and walks into the living room.) "I'm sorry, Mom. You're right, I wasn't taking 'no' for an answer. Maybe David can come over and watch a video."

Rachel: (Tears well up in her eyes. This is the kind of experience that she's been having since Brian got back. The old patterns start, but then she, and often Brian, act in completely different ways.) "I love you, son." (She hugs him and kisses him, which feels wonderful to both of them.)

Exclusive individual boundaries were Rachel resisting her impulse to capitulate and Brian confronting his angry *"Screw her, I should run away."* Both recognized the violence of their impulses and did not surrender to destructive thought and action.

Inclusive individual boundaries were Rachel forcing herself to ask Brian for details of his plans, and Brian making himself apologize for being rude. Both insisted on including healthy behaviors they were resisting.

An inclusive interpersonal boundary was Rachel telling Brian to cool down and then apologize. She directed him toward healthy activity and then walked away, refusing further defensive dialog.

Exclusive interpersonal boundaries were Rachel refusing to let Brian go out and taking his computer away as a consequence of him swearing at her. She would not allow these behaviors without protest and consequence.

Defensive states make boundaries difficult.

Defensive states involve very little empathy. This makes it hard to feel into ourselves and others effectively and discern appropriate and proportionate responses to distressing events and thoughts.

I've found that mothers can become so accustomed to attending to others that they have diminished ability to feel into themselves, thus making them more prone to passive aggressive errors of tolerating pain rather than acting assertively. When Brian pressured Rachel to let him go to David's house, she had a reflexive impulse to say "yes" to intimidation. Because she had learned to attune to herself, she realized she was being coerced and remembered her resolve to set boundaries when she felt pushed.

Similarly, I've often found fathers to be so focused on solving problems, or on combatting infuriating challenges to their authority, that they can overreact, impose unrealistically harsh consequences ("You're grounded for a month!"), or lose their abilities to slow things down, consult with others, or attune to children and spouse. Here's Harry walking in on the above scene, just as Rachel and Brian are finishing their conversation:

Harry: "What's going on?"

Rachel: "Brian wanted to go out with David, and I ..."

Harry: (Alarmed, he remembers picking Brian and David up at the police station two years ago.) "No way! What are you thinking? He's only been home five months, and …"

Brian: (He sets an exclusive boundary for his father.) "Cut it out, Dad. We've already worked it out."

Harry: (He registers the disgusted expressions on both their faces, and feels ashamed. *"I said in therapy that I wouldn't jump to conclusions, and I just did."*) "Oops. Uh, I'm sorry. So, you've, uh, already worked it out?" (This lame, but endearing recovery cracks up both Rachel and Brian.)

Rachel: "Good job backing off. You get a hug too." (As she hugs him, all three feel good.)

A parent with an impulsive boundary-setting style often benefits from consulting and processing before action; in other words, attuning with others. A parent who blanks out often benefits from checking into his or her own sensations, feelings, thoughts, and impulses before action; attuning with self. Either way, the questions of what serves the highest good and what is *my* responsibility in this moment are more likely to be addressed.

Boundaries with our lover.

Rachel found Harry attractive when he responded positively to her disgusted look and Brian's confrontation. Harry found Rachel attractive as she stood up to Brian instead of capitulating to his anger and hugged both of them when they supported her boundaries. A relationship without effective boundaries inevitably has problems with erotic polarity, since the feminine partner can feel unsafe and unseen and a masculine partner can feel frustrated and emasculated. If a spouse can't (or won't) set boundaries for self or others, they lose credibility and visibility to their partner. Effective boundaries help our partners feel into us and know what attracts and repulses, what feels right and wrong. The next day, Harry and Rachel are discussing the incident in a conjoint therapy session:

Keith: "Good job resolving it. You both set great boundaries."

Harry: "I didn't set any boundaries. I just put my foot in my mouth."

Keith: "Sure you did. You set a boundary for yourself. How often in the past have you backed off when Brian's told you to 'cut it out?'"

Harry: "He was right this time." (Rachel rolls her eyes.) "What? He was right this time."

Rachel: "He's been right before. You just listened to him this time."

Harry: "Well it really helped that you didn't cave in like you used to."

Keith: (They're getting irritated without considering why. Both have been injured repetitively by the other's difficulties with boundaries. Harry's had to watch the kids, and especially Brian, walk all over Rachel for years. Rachel's had to endure Harry's impulsive, over-the-top bullying ever since Brian was two and started challenging authority.) "What are you feeling right now?"

Rachel: "Frustrated."

Harry: "Pissed."

Keith: (I want to encourage them to attune.) "That's interesting. You had an episode that ended better than usual. Both of you admired the other's responses, and now you're getting upset. What do you think is happening?"

Harry: "I'm not used to us being different. I guess it's just a habit to get mad when we talk about parenting. I'm used to Rachel being a pushover with the kids and mad at me." (He turns to Rachel.) "I'm sorry. You handled the situation with Brian, and then me, really well."

Rachel: (The feminine grows best in the presence of loving praise.) "I did set a good boundary for Brian. I felt like letting him go over to David's, but I knew he was jamming me and I held firm. Then I didn't stay mad at you after you butted in."

Keith: "That was an important part; the inclusive boundary. You insisted on loving Harry up when he responded well. In the old days you didn't realize how important it is to him for you to touch him and love him." (She smiles warmly at Harry.)

Harry: (He reaches out and strokes her arm.) "It makes all the difference."

Keith: "One of the great blessings of a healthy, mature marriage is the opportunity to insist on including your spouse in important decisions and discernments, and having the standard of processing decisions and conflicts until they feel beautiful and good to both of you. If you have the strength and care to insist on those things for yourself, and to advocate those things with your spouse, you go through life with the advantage of two people's wisdom. I believe this gives you an edge in dealing with everything."

Feeling both powerful and respectful of your partner strengthens the marital relationship. Knowing and being true to your masculine and feminine responsibilities supports erotic polarity. As Harry recognized her efforts and praised her, Rachel felt known and claimed, and safe and loved. As Rachel showed him her pleasure through her body (with her warm smile), Harry's mature depth was evoked and reinforced. Where they were repelling each other earlier when they were beginning to constellate the old resentments, they were now attracting each other with feminine radiance and masculine depth of consciousness. Erotic polarity requires effective inclusive and exclusive boundaries practiced by both partners.

Positive and negative drama.

Each life is a soap opera, with lots of characters and emotionally charged action. Drama is the nature of human existence. Nobody's development is perfect, but everybody has good times and everybody has their share of unavoidable problems, disasters, and random losses.

We usually have a lot of influence over whether things are getting better or getting worse. Healthy boundaries tend to make negative things slow down and positive things more likely. This is positive drama. Being unable or unwilling to set healthy boundaries tends to make everything worse. This is negative drama. Both positive and negative drama can be either pleasurable or painful. What distinguishes them is that positive drama includes the struggle and effort that's often required to attune and set boundaries, while negative drama results from indulging destructive impulses.

An example of painful positive drama might be me taking a fall from my mountain bike, breaking my clavicle, and then meticulously going through all the necessary steps to heal. These steps involve intense experiences for me, my family, my clients, and various health practitioners, but, if we are in community dealing with this crisis, we all grow from our involvement.

An example of painful negative drama might be me falling from my bike, breaking my clavicle, ignoring doctor's orders and being difficult as an invalid with my family. These bad decisions lead to interpersonal conflict and physical complications.

An example of pleasurable positive drama is attending your daughter's dance recital and being moved to tears by her solo performance in front of an enraptured audience.

An example of pleasurable negative drama is a husband having a secret affair with a co-worker. They intensely enjoy their romantic infatuation, but this pleasure eventually comes at the cost of many people's suffering.

Negative drama can shift to positive drama as soon as a participant decides to attune. In the affair example, either husband or co-worker could, at any moment, shift from negative to positive drama by resisting destructive impulses, refusing to continue the affair, and doing their best to help everyone clean up the mess.

Positive drama de-escalates defenses, negative drama escalates defenses.

This last example illustrates how setting healthy boundaries de-escalates defenses. Allowing an affair to continue tends to keep creating more suffering. Stopping an affair (or just acknowledging and effectively dealing with a distracting attraction) requires effort and results in emotionally charged experiences for everyone involved; but these emotionally charged experiences tend to move participants toward appropriate emotional charge, compassionate perspectives, and healthy impulses, rather than deeper into defensive states.

Just as we cheer on a movie hero when he makes good decisions and groan when he makes bad decisions, we feel moral strength and internal beauty when we implement good decisions, even those that involve suffering, and feel internal distress and collapse when we indulge destructive impulses. Healthy inclusive and exclusive boundaries ultimately serve love.

The boundary food chain.

The easiest boundaries are those that we set with pleasure for ourselves and with mutual attunement with others. An example is the following exchange between Brian and his friend Damon. They are out on the ocean bluffs near Brian's house, flying radio controlled gliders. Damon's plane just crashed and is temporarily unusable:

Brian: "Do you want me to call my dad to pick us up?"

Damon: (He's bummed that he can't fly anymore, but it's a perfect day and he doesn't want to go home.) "No, it's OK. You go ahead, I'll just hang."

Brian: (He feels something is not right, and it's awkward that they can't fly together. The game they love is trying to crash each other's plane, and now Damon can't play.) "I want to stay, but I want you to fly too."

Damon: "I'll bet I can take it higher than you."

Brian: "We'll take turns."

Brian noticed his friend was unhappy and insisted on a solution that felt good to both boys. Damon participated gladly. These boundaries are so smooth that it's hard to see that they are boundaries at all.

The hardest individual boundaries are those that go against our most powerful defensive impulses, such as the alcoholic refusing the drink, the tired child refusing to stay up late playing his beloved video games, or the exercise phobic person forcing herself into the gym.

The hardest interpersonal boundaries are those we set in the face of another's defensive resistance or incomprehension. Parents encounter this all the time:

Harry: (He's at the coffee shop with Hannah and Albert. Hannah gets hot chocolate, and Albert wants a frappachino.) "Sorry son, it's 3:00 and there's enough caffeine in that drink to keep you up all night. Maybe a decaffeinated one?"

Albert: "No, I want the regular one. Come on, it's still the afternoon."

Harry: "Sorry son, it's not a good idea. Get the decaffeinated one."

Albert: "You're being so unfair. You're getting a coffee drink, and Hannah got what she wanted."

Harry: "I wouldn't let her have a caffeinated drink, and, God help me, I have enough tolerance built up for caffeine that I'll sleep fine tonight."

Albert: "It's not fair!"

Harry: (He realizes Albert's too upset to cooperate.) "Hot chocolate, decaffeinated frappachino, something else with no caffeine, or nothing. Your choice."

Albert: "Nothing!"

Harry: "I'm sorry, son. Why don't you wait out front while Hannah and I get our drinks?" (Albert storms out, furious and in tears.)

Harry tried unsuccessfully for immediate repair after he and Hannah got their order, and later, after Albert calmed down, they had a healing talk. Like most good parents, Harry used a respectful tone and clear principles during the incident to support Albert's sense of dignity and fairness. This made repair easier later and helped Albert understand how his father was trying to do right. In the store though, Harry had to set boundaries in the face of Albert's anger and incomprehension.

Part of being a great parent to our children and a great lover to our spouse is maintaining an attitude that we do our best to set necessary boundaries respectfully and collaboratively and that we'll reluctantly set unilateral boundaries if we must. If we believe that we're always growing in these capacities, it makes it easier to tolerate everyone's failures and collapses and easier to move up the boundary food chain toward more respectful, affectionate, and collaborate boundary setting.

1. Siegal (2005)

2. Witt (2005)

10

What if I have no idea what anybody is feeling?

A successful businessman named Jed comes into my office for the first time:

Jed: "My wife said I had to come. She says I'm angry all the time, but I don't feel angry. I feel fine."

Keith: "What are you feeling in your body at this moment?"

Jed: "I don't know."

Keith: "Are you hot, cold, tense, relaxed, happy, sad, angry, joyful, ashamed, or surprised?"

Jed: "I have no idea."

Conscious awareness is a slippery thing. What are you feeling in your stomach at this moment? Full, empty, relaxed, tense, satisfied, unresolved, or something else? All these feelings, sensations, or concepts can be associated with what you're feeling in your stomach. Maybe you feel nothing at all. This exercise can be done with what you feel in your heart, abdomen, feet, legs, pelvis, solar plexus, throat, jaw, face, head, arms, and hands. With practice, you can focus on any part of your body and develop increasing sensitivity to the sensations of that area, the emotions you associate with those sensations, and the thoughts and impulses that typically arise from these experiences. These sensations, feelings, thoughts, and impulses will be either more or less attractive and welcome to you. Joy is usually welcome; despair is usually repulsive. Caring thoughts often seem beautiful and good; mean thoughts often ugly and bad.

Neuroscience has shown that our existence is drenched with emotions[1] and that our bodies are always communicating to us via sensation (for instance, our gut and heart react to our experience and send messages via our vagus nerves to our brain[2]), but we can be blocked in our conscious awareness. I've found that focusing on sensation is an effective first step to expanding emotional awakening. Jed and I continue:

Keith: "Are you relaxed or tense?"

Jed: "A little tense, I guess."

Keith: "What emotion do you associate with tension?"

Jed: "I don't understand the question."

Keith: "Does tension suggest joy, anger, anxiety, sadness, shame, or grief?"

Jed: "Anxiety, I guess."

Keith: "What might you be anxious about at this moment?"

Jed: "Nothing. There's nothing to be anxious about."

Keith: "Have you ever been in therapy before?"

Jed: "No."

Keith: "Often new experiences are a little scary and uncomfortable, especially at first."

Jed: "I really don't know what to do here, or what you want."

Keith: "Do you think that might make you a little tense and anxious?"

Jed: "Yeah, I guess."

Keith: "How would you like to feel?"

Jed: "What kind of a question is that? Of course I want to feel good."

Keith: "You sound irritated."

Jed: "It's kind of a stupid question. Who doesn't want to feel good?"

Keith: "If you could engage in practices that would develop your power to feel good much more often, would you be interested in learning them?"

Jed: "This sounds like airy-fairy, new age, Dr. Feelgood crap to me."

Keith: "Now you sound angry."

Jed: "I'm not angry. You sound just like my wife. She's always telling me how angry I am."

Keith: "That must be irritating."

Jed: "You have no idea."

One of the most inspiring findings of attachment research is that adults can change their personal narrative; their life story about how they've grown, who they are, and where they're going.[3] Maybe the story you tell yourself is you don't feel much, or you don't notice what you feel, or you feel bad, or what you feel is irrelevant. You can change that story. The story, "I don't feel much." can change to "I'm feeling more all the time."

If we embrace the reality that we're always writing our own story, an important question is, "What direction do I want to grow?" If we choose an ideal and direct ourselves to grow toward it, we will transform over time to become progressively more an embodiment of that ideal. This is an evolutionary capacity of our human brains and nervous systems, the ability to transform and reinterpret our past, present, and future in directions that we consciously choose.

Direction and momentum.

Neuroscience tells us that anytime we enter a state of consciousness, we are practicing that state and increasing the chances of entering it again.[4] We are constellating and solidifying neural networks. This means that each decision we make creates momentum in a direction of personal evolution. If you choose kindness a thousand times and your neighbor chooses kindness twice, who is more likely to choose kindness in a given situation? If you choose emotional violence a thousand times and your neighbor compassion a thousand times, who is more likely to choose violence or compassion in a given situation?

If we want a life of empathic sensitivity to ourselves and others, and consistent good decisions, then each time we reach for these things we create direction and momentum toward attunement as a reflexive response, until eventually it becomes our habitual choice, or a personality trait.

Attunement doesn't necessarily mean that we are aware of what we and others feel, think, and want all the time. Attunement is simply considering what we and others feel, think, and want, and reaching for caring thought and action. The organizing principle of this process is to do our best to discern and embrace truth, beauty, and goodness. Each time we attempt this, we are creating direction and momentum toward consistent attunement.

Find a channel to inner awareness, and use it.

A good place to start developing sensitivity to inner experience is to find an access point, a channel into the interior, that feels authentic and then to consistently practice utilizing that channel over time. Focusing on sensation is an effective technique, but most of us need a rationale to attend to sensation that feels consistent with our worldview.

Jed's mother was three when Germany invaded Poland. She and her family fled the Natzis and spent the next ten years enduring incredible dangers and hardships before they had a secure existence in Michigan. The legacy of this odyssey for Jed's mother was to be psychologically frozen and emotionally unresponsive, leaving her dismissive of her children's emotional needs and demands. Jed's father was a hard-working traveling salesman who loved his family, but was distant from all of them. Jed grew into a self-contained, competent, rational electrical engineer whose attachment style was dismissive and avoidant. He rarely considered what he was feeling, and thought it was "weak" to dwell on inner experience. Jed only entered therapy when his wife, Stella, set the boundary that he get treatment or leave the house. My challenge was to inspire him to wake up to his body, sensations, emotions, and yearnings.

As the session unfolds, I observe that Jed's developmental center is rational. He is equally contemptuous of conformist religious or social beliefs (he speaks disparagingly about religion being "the opiate of the masses") and pluralistic, egalitarian, multiculturalism (he's outraged that some of his classmates at M.I.T. were admitted because they were minorities).

People's worldviews tend to grow from conformist, to rational, to pluralistic, to integral.[5] Until they stabilize at integral (which is characterized by an appreciation for most perspectives), people tend to find other worldviews irritating. Rational worldviews tend to appear in adolescence when teenagers' cognitive abilities expand and they are reaching for adult identities. As they grow, they can develop towards group oriented, non-hierarchical, multicultural pluralistic worldviews, and beyond to other worldviews, or stay rational for a lifetime.[6] Individuals such as Jed, with primarily rational worldviews, tend to be individualistic, hungry for position on merit-based hierarchies, and respond positively to scientific data. Science is the language I use to connect with him:

> Keith: "Research has shown us that consistent self-reflection enhances immune function, increases cardiovascular health, improves relationships, and increases a sense of well-being."[7]

> Jed: "I'd like to see that research."

Keith: (I feel a warm sense of satisfaction. I feel attuned to Jed. He has a masculine essence that can be engaged by loving challenge.) "I'll give you the references before you leave. You have children, right?"

Jed: "Yes, two girls, Patty and Ruthie. They're two and four."

Keith: "How do you get along with them?"

Jed: "What do you mean?"

Keith: "Do you hang out? Do you play together? What kinds of activities do you do with them?"

Jed: (Shifting uncomfortably.) "Stella does most of the parent stuff. I work hard, and my job uses a lot of time."

Keith: "That's too bad for you and them. Studies show that kids would rather play with their father at those ages than with their mother.[8] It also improves marital relationships when fathers play with their children."

Jed: "I never know what to do."

Keith: (Here is a channel presenting itself; an intersection between his scientific self and his desire for better relationships.) "In the next week I suggest you observe and record what kinds of play the girls engage in with Stella and each other. Their favorites will be the games where they smile, laugh, and seem the happiest, and the ones where they continue to stay involved without being distracted in other directions. You can bring your notes into our next session."

Jed: "I can do that."

Over the next several weeks, Jed discovered that his two-year-old, Patti, liked to play peek-a-boo, and that four-year-old Ruthie enjoyed playing tea party and a monster game where she and Jed took turns playing the monster. I encouraged him to spend time each day playing with the girls, and to pay attention to what he felt during the play. He reported that it felt "good" to play with the girls, but that he was also often bored with some of the games.

The following exchange is from our seventh session. By now Jed has come to enjoy therapy and is less hostile and more open during sessions. He doesn't realize how much his openness is a function of my attunement in the face of his defensive closures. I don't bite when he makes insulting or dismissive comments; I keep bringing our combined focus onto his sensations, emotions, thoughts, and impulses; and I stay attuned to him during his frequent disconnects and subtle attacks. Throughout all this I keep beating the drum about how research supports self-reflection, empathy, and caring action as major sources of physical, emotional, and relational health for everybody in a family. I also keep patiently pointing out how his emotions reveal themselves outside of his awareness:

Keith: "How's it going at home?"

Jed: "Better. Stella is less bitchy, and I'm having more fun with the girls. Ruthie said, 'I love my Daddy,' in pre-school, and her teacher told me."

Keith: "How did it feel to hear that?"

Jed: "Great."

Keith: "You seem to be getting a sense about how emotion permeates every aspect of your life at home."

Jed: "Yeah, I guess. Though Stella keeps getting mad at me for no reason."

Keith: "What're some examples?"

Jed: "She asked me how she looked in a dress she bought, and I told her that her legs were too fat for short skirts. Then when she got way too mad, I told her she was acting irrationally, and she told me to 'go fuck myself.'"

Keith: (Laughing.) "That's getting mad at you for no reason? Come on, you're kidding, right? Telling your wife her legs are too fat, and then telling her she's irrational for getting furious, are like trying to put out a grease fire with a bucket of gasoline."

Jed: (Laughing in spite of himself.) "Well, OK. It wasn't so clear at the time."

Keith: "What are you feeling in your body at this moment?"

Jed: "Mostly relaxed, though I'm a little embarrassed about what I said to Stella."

Keith: "You notice how you're clearer about what you feel than you were in our first session?"

Jed: "Now that you mention it, yes. Stella's said the same thing. She said she feels more connected. We even had sex."

Keith: "Great, that's the first time in several months. How was it?"

Jed: "We enjoyed it."

Keith: "How do you know? What did you feel that let you know it was enjoyable, and how could you tell Stella enjoyed it?"

Jed: "I felt excited. I liked how she felt. She had an orgasm, you know, moved and made sounds. She said she liked it afterwards."

Keith: "Did you enjoy her pleasure? Feminine pleasure, particularly in the form of movement, breath, and sound tends to nourish masculine people."

Jed: "I enjoyed it a lot."

Keith: "This is an example of you erotically attuning to her. You felt into yourself, her, and connected with the intent of supporting mutual pleasure and love."

Jed: "You make it sound easy. I really don't know how it happened."

Keith: "The more you practice feeling into both of your sensations, emotions, thoughts, and impulses, and reaching to do what creates love, the better you'll get at it."

Jed: "She still gets mad at me all the time."

Keith: "Maybe it's time for her to come into the sessions."

Jed: "She said she would. I'll ask her."

Jed is a responsible person who is dedicated to his family and work. He's now in an awakening process where he's bending his considerable reasoning skills and cognitive capacity toward addressing his emotional blocks and barriers. His ability to reason and consider scientific data is being used as a channel to support inner awareness of sensation, emotion, thought, and impulse, and, in the process, he's becoming more sensitive to others' inner experience (as well as creating and strengthening connections between his linear, logical, linguistic left hemisphere and his kinesthetic, non-linear, intuitive right hemisphere). He is changing his personal narrative from "I have no idea what I'm feeling" to "I'm getting better at knowing what I and others feel."

We learn self-reflection in stages.

Charles Darwin, in his last book, asserted that all mammals experience the same emotions[9] (what Daniel Siegal calls "categorical emotions" to distinguish them from our reflexive "yum" and "yuck" "primary emotions"[10]). These include happiness, surprise, sadness, anger, shame, fear, and disgust. We all experience these emotions regularly, and, if our bodies and brains were monitored, they would show the characteristic endocrine shifts and neurological activations that are typical of such states. Feeling an emotion and *being consciously aware* of an emotion are different things.

Conscious awareness, as reflected by our ability to have explicit memories (where I can remember yesterday and anticipate tomorrow), seems to blossom at around eighteen months of age as our hippocampus (a brain area associated with explicit memory) comes online (though it is not fully functional till around age five). As children's nervous systems are taught how to grow by interfacing with parents' nervous systems, children's perspectives and understanding are shaped by interpersonal experience. I both learn that happiness is called "happiness" and whether I am more or less acceptable when I'm happy from my interpersonal experience with my family. How I make sense of such experiences and discoveries is the beginning of my personal narrative, or life story.

When Jed's little girls approached him happily or angrily and were met with incomprehension and awkward stiffness, they were receiving a critical message about being in a happy or angry state. Not surprisingly, this was consistent with the messages that Jed got from his emotionally resistant mother when he was small and approached her while feeling something strongly. Humans have mirror neurons in their frontal cortex that mirror other's *states of mind.*[11] This is a biological base of empathy, and one way that all children absorb information, nervous system to nervous system. When parents consciously monitor emotional exchanges and direct and explain them to support healthy growth, development become a more mindful and conscious process. An example is the following exchange between Jed's wife, Stella, and their two girls, Patty and Ruthie:

Stella: (The girls are playing with colored blocks in the living room.) "Time for bath."

Ruthie: "I want to play blocks." (Patty chimes in with, "Pay bocks!")

Stella: "Five more minutes, and then bath time. I'll set the timer." (She sets the timer and goes off to run the bath. Five minutes later the timer goes off and she's back.) "Time for bath."

Ruthie: "No! I want to play blocks." (She begins crying as Stella picks her up, carries her into the bath, and starts taking off her clothes.)

Stella: "You're frustrated because you want to play blocks and it's bath time." (Patty again contributes, "Pay bocks!" Stella looks at her and responds.)

"You're frustrated because you were having fun playing blocks with your sister and it's bath time."

Ruthie: (She relaxes a little as she's lowered into the warm water, but she's still upset.) "I'm mad."

Stella: "Yes, you're mad at me because I said you have to take your bath."(Ruthie nods, but the pleasurable bath and her splashy little sister soon distract her.)

Later that night, Stella tells them the story of their day.

Stella: "We got up, ate breakfast, and took Ruthie to preschool. Patty and I went shopping and then went to the zoo."

Pattie: "Zoo, elfants!"

Stella: "Yes, you like the elephants. Then we picked up Ruthie and went home to play. We had hot dogs for dinner. After dinner, we played with the colored blocks, and you got mad when we had to stop and take a bath."

Ruthie: "I got mad at Mommie."

Stella: "You and Patty both got mad at me, but then you had a nice bath."

Stella is helping the girls identify and accept what they're feeling. "You're frustrated," "you like the elephants," "you got mad at me," are all examples of feeling into the girls and teaching them how to identify and accept what they experience. She does this by attuning to herself and the girls, explaining their emotions as they go about their day, and telling them a coherent story of their day at bedtime. This helps the girls identify and accept what they feel, and develop their own capacities for coherent narrative. In addition, this process supports the integration of the girls' non-verbal, emotionally/kinesthetically oriented right brain hemispheres with their verbal, linguistic, linear, cause and effect, left hemispheres.[12] Such integration has been associated with secure attachment, emotional awareness, and superior self-reflecting skills in children.[13]

From first conscious awareness through pre-school, children relate to parents as infallible beings with God-like powers. As we explored earlier, if parents don't embrace this role of power-God, the child can take it on and essentially run the family. The stories preschoolers tell themselves are often magical, in that people can do magical things just like comic book heroes.

At around ages five or six, children begin to have increased internal desires to conform to rules and be accepted as members of the family and other important groups. They recognize that their parents don't personally have God-like powers, but they do have control of, or influence over, huge forces like cars, schools, and TVs. This conformist stage continues through elementary school years where concrete rules of all sorts are important to children.[14] The stories these children tell themselves are often mythical, in that there are forces like "God," or "the Government" who espouse rules that have significant, even sacred importance and that these forces can be influenced by authority figures, petitionary prayer, or other forms of intervention.

As young teens develop the formal operational cognitive capacities to hold opposing concepts and inhabit "what if" situations (what Piaget called "formal operational" thought), they increasingly rely on personal opinions, more flexible and relative moral values, and peer standards. They are developing adult identities, which, hopefully, are being integrated into coherent life narratives. They can take into account different perspectives, and more individual, idiosyncratic value systems. An important caveat with teens is recognizing that their brains do not fully mature till age twenty-six. For example, teenagers have more difficulty correctly interpreting emotions from facial expressions than do mature adults.

Secure attachment styles support healthy growth in all these worldviews, while insecure attachment styles can block, warp, or interfere with healthy development.[15]

Patty and Ruthie have secure attachment styles with Stella, heading toward having secure/autonomous adult attachment styles as they grow up. One fly in their developmental ointment is Jed's dismissive attitude towards inner experience, combined with Stella and Jed's conflicted marital relationship.

Married couples shape each other's minds.

When we choose lovers, we tend to pick people who complement our dreams and our wounds. These people will feel "familiar" and attractive in subtle ways no one fully understands, but are almost certainly linked to our family-of-origin experiences, our defensive structures, and our attachment styles. Since all communication is collaborative and complementary (we have to cooperate to have mutually comprehensible dialog), we direct each other's attention to some extent each time we interact. Attention determines where and how energy and information flow happen in brains, which creates and shapes neural networks. Couples evoke complementary states, which are reinforced each time they are activated. Thus, when we engage our partners, we shape each other's minds, a process that can continue long after a relationship ends through our innate capacity to "internalize" working models of important figures.

A fascinating finding from attachment research is that some individuals who had insecure attachment as infants, or believed that they had insecure attachment, had achieved a secure attachment style (meaning having a coherent narrative in which their lives made sense in the past, present, and future) as adults. These people were characterized as having "earned" secure attachment, and they almost universally attributed their status to at least one *successful intimate relationship* with a family member, friend, teacher, or lover.[16]

As adults, marriage is arguably the most potent and influential relationship that many of us will have. This relationship can support growth and change or codependently lock us into rigid defensive habits. Since entering a state means we're practicing that state, healthy and unhealthy relating styles tend to amplify their developmental effects over time. In other words, couples repeatedly evoke and reinforce the best and/or worst in each other and maintain those states through complementary communication through the duration of their relationship and beyond.

Stella, her older brother, and their younger sister were raised by a single, alcoholic mother who worked hard and loved her children, but who tended to be maudlin and intrusive, or shut down and distant, when she drank. Stella's father saw her and her siblings on alternate weekends and was a fun guy when he showed up, but seemed to feel little responsibility for his children's development, and would avoid them if they complained.

Starting at seventeen, Stella had several unstable relationships in which one man cheated and another turned out to be an alcoholic. When she met Jed at work, his solid, unflappable presence was attractive and welcome. During the romantic infatuation stage of their relationship, Stella thought that she had finally met her perfect man.

After their wedding, problems started. Stella found that when emotions got charged, Jed either left or became logical and robotic. First playfully, and then with real venom, she began calling him "Mr. Spock" after the *Star Trek* alien who felt no emotion and organized his life with pure logic.

Her pregnancies and births were welcome distractions. Jed was solid, a good provider, and competent around the house. Her intense emotional involvement with the children compensated for the emotional desert she felt with him. He became more cynical and distant as she became more contemptuous and dismissive of him as an emotionally incompetent man. She lost interest in sex, and, for Jed, this had been his lifeline to her. He consistently refused her offers to go to therapy with him, or her encouragement for him to go alone. What finally pushed her over the edge was his inability to be warm and cuddly with the girls. Like many mothers who were raised in a codependent, alcoholic system, she felt more moved to set boundaries in service of others than in service of herself. Believing her children were suffering from disconnection from Jed was what finally empowered her to draw the line: "Get therapy or leave." The following is from our first conjoint session:

> Keith: (After greeting them and spending some time finding out about Stella's history, I ask about their relationship.) "Stella, how have things been with Jed since he started therapy?"

> Stella: (She firmly believes that all their problems are a result of Jed being "shut down," and she's so used to being the expert on emotion, psychology, and relationship that she unconsciously assumes a collegial air, as if we are both therapists discussing a mutual case. She is completely unaware of how demeaning this feels to Jed, though at this stage in his work all he feels is vague irritation as she analyses him.) "I think Jed is coming along fine. He's much better with the girls. They play and both of them look forward to him getting home. He's reading to them at night. He also hasn't fought with me so much."

> Keith: "How is your relationship with each other?"

> Stella: "It still needs a lot of work. Jed has no idea what it's like to be a woman."

> Keith: "What's your reaction as Stella talks, Jed."

> Jed: "Ask her. She knows everything."

> Stella: "Now, Jed …"

> Keith: "OK, you're angry. What is Stella doing that pisses you off?"

> Jed: "I'm not angry." (Stella gives me an "I told you so" look.) "Maybe I'm irritated."

> Keith: "Alright, what irritates you?"

> Jed: "She just seems to know everything. It's always me that's screwed up."

> Stella: "I'm willing to talk about my feelings. I'm willing to have therapy."

> Jed: "I'm in therapy now."

Keith: "Stella, what's valid about Jed's resentments?"

Stella: (This confuses her.) "What do you mean?"

Keith: "Jed is suggesting that you think all your problems are a result of him, and that you have no part in your conflicts. What's valid about that?"

Stella: (Speaking slowly, and visibly reaching for self-awareness.) "I guess I do blame him. I know I must contribute, but I don't see how. I try to communicate. I try to be open and talk about things that are important. It's just that Jed doesn't seem interested."

Keith: "I've found that married couples know each other better than anyone. Jed, what's Stella's part in your problems?"

Jed: (Very reluctantly, he begins to talk. He can express reflexive passive-aggressive digs relatively easily, but he has inhibitions about consciously criticizing an important intimate feminine partner that go all the way back to his mother locking him in his room for the mildest complaint.) "You always seem impatient and angry with me. You don't think I have anything useful to say about parenting, and we have practically no sex."

Stella: "You try to have enough energy for sex after chasing two little girls around all day. I'm not angry all the time. You just don't notice when I feel close. You don't notice when I feel anything."

Keith: "I can hear your yearning for Jed to know you. It's so important to feel 'felt.'"

Stella: "Yes. That's it. I want to feel 'felt.'" (She looks expectantly at Jed.)

Keith: "Jed, look at Stella, feel into your heart, feel into her heart, and tell her what you think is going on inside her."

Jed: (This is very hard for him, but we've been working at practicing attunement skills for two months now.) "I think you're frustrated, and are afraid I won't be able to do it, you know, have an emotional connection with you."

Stella: "Why yes. That's real close." (She looks at him as if she's seeing him for the first time in the session.)

Keith: "How does Stella's reaction feel, Jed?"

Jed: (Looking in her eyes.) "Good; like when we first met, and she thought I was great." (This brings tears to Stella's eyes.)

Stella and Jed need many such moments to develop secure/autonomous attachment. Jed also yearns to feel "felt," but is only barely aware of his yearning. He unconsciously translates it into more rational, concrete wishes such as, "I want her to be less angry," "I want to have sex more often," or "I want her to respect my opinions."

A central aspect for both in feeling "felt" is each understanding their different natures as more masculine or feminine beings. I explain this to them three sessions later, after they have had a chance to practice creating mutually attuned moments in a variety of circumstances:

> Keith: "Stella, do you notice how Jed wants you to view him as a successful husband and father?" (She nods.) "And Jed, do you notice how Stella wants you to create more connection, caring, and love with her and the girls?" (He nods.) "A masculine person's life tends to cycle through success, failure, success, failure, success, and so on until death. A feminine person's life tends cycle through love is happening, love is not happening, love is happening, and so on until death. Even though everyone has both masculine and feminine aspects, these basic rhythms will have different significance to more feminine or more masculine people."[17]

> Stella: "Is that why Jed gets so mad when I tell him I don't like something. It makes him feel like a failure?"

> Keith: "Ask Jed."

> Stella: (She looks at him.) "Well?"

> Jed: "Absolutely. I do my best, make a little mistake, and then you think I've totally screwed up. I do feel like a failure when that happens."

> Stella: "That's not what I mean. I just notice how things can be better."

> Keith: "The feminine is never satisfied for long. In a feminine moment you are a wide open channel of emotion, fully in the present, and visibly reacting with pleasure when things go well, and suffering when things so poorly. Feminine people often notice how things could be more beautiful, or love could happen better. As long as you show Jed your pleasure and satisfaction in the moments when he makes an effort, your regular dissatisfaction and yearning for positive change is more tolerable and is even a resource for your family in creating more beauty and love. If you get so frustrated that you never show pleasure at his positive efforts, the message he gets as a man is that he's always failing."

Stella: "I don't want that. I think Jed's doing wonderfully." (Jed visibly relaxes and smiles as he hears this.)

Keith: "Then keep noticing his efforts and loving him up when you see them." (Both laugh at this.)

Jed: "But what do I do to make Stella feel that love's happening?"

Keith: (This is an important and difficult question. Jed, as a more masculine person, wants specific solutions. Feminine people often value processing over solutions. That's fine, but it's often hard for a masculine person to realize that the solution to a problem with his wife is for her to feel known and claimed, and safe and loved. 'Known' means attuning to both of you, and helping her feel 'felt.' 'Claimed' means communicating acceptance of her, and desire to be with her, no matter what she's feeling or thinking. 'Safe' means having a standard of being emotionally non-violent whenever you're around her or the kids, no matter how angry or hurt you are, and never trying to rationalize or justify repulsive violent attitudes or behaviors. 'Loved' means doing the things that please and open her, and noticing the things that hurt and close her, and committing to always be working toward more of the former and less of the latter. This is way too much information to impart all at once, so I offer him an organizing principle that touches all these bases.) "Keep attuning to yourself, Stella, and your girls. Feeling into yourself and others with positive intent supports love."

Jed: (Unconsciously back on success/failure.) "I keep forgetting or getting distracted. It's so hard to remember to focus on what we're feeling, thinking, and wanting, and talk to Stella about it. I'm not very good at the feeling stuff."

Keith: "Remember your new story, 'I'm getting better all the time at feeling into myself and my family.' You don't have to do it perfectly. Success is just making regular efforts and regular progress." (Stella nods at this, and Jed notices and relaxes.)

Where masculine people can block all emotion except the desires for justice and success, feminine people can block anger and pleasure. Stella's story about herself was that she was emotionally aware but never got the love she wanted. This tended to make her numb to the sensual pleasures of observing and embracing Jed's efforts. Part of her awakening was learning to feel the pleasure in her body when Jed worked at attunement, and to show him this pleasure through expression, movement, breath, and verbal acknowledgement.

If we attune, we can tell whether we're opening or closing our partners, and happy couples use these perceptions to grow in being their best selves. When both Jed and Stella were doing their work, they were evoking and reinforcing more integrated neural networks in each other's brains that attuned more readily, loved more easily, and were more consistent with their emerging transformative life narratives; this is what great parents and great lovers tend to do.

1. Siegal (1999)

2. Porges (2006)

3. Siegal (2003)

4. Siegal (1999)

5. Beck (1996)

6. Wilber (2003)

7. Siegal (2005)

8. Gottman (2005)

9. Darwin (1872)

10. Siegal (1999)

11. Siegal (2005)

12. *Ibid*

13. *Ibid*

14. Wilber (2003)

15. Siegal (1999)

16. *Ibid*

17. Deida (2004)

11

Addiction

One study found that fifty percent of Americans either were addicted to drugs or alcohol or had a close relative who was addicted. One in three children live in a home where alcoholism is present.[1] Having a chemically dependent person in the family means that the family system adjusts to the addiction. This adjustment usually moves simultaneously in two general directions: toward codependence and toward cleaner boundaries. Codependence means accommodating and abetting unhealthy behavior in some way, an inevitable result of living with addiction. Cleaner boundaries are a result of family members slowly waking up to their participation in sick behavior and progressively deciding to refuse to actively or passively support it. There is usually movement in both of these directions until one predominates, resulting eventually in the addict entering recovery, being excluded from the family, dying, or the family surrendering to the pressure to be codependent, leading them to tolerate and indirectly support the addictive behavior.

Anyone who has grown up with an addicted parent, been married to an addict, had a child become an addict, or who is in recovery for addiction (sometimes, all of the above) can attest to the nightmare of what addiction does to families. Like cancer, it can debilitate the whole system until everyone is corrupted.

The signature defensive strategies of an addict are denial ("I have no problem") and rationalization ("I drink/use because I'm happy, sad, tired, anxious, angry, celebrating, consoling, being social, alleviating stress, etc.).

The signature defensive strategies of an addict's family member are denial, rescue, and persecution.

Common examples of denial are "Mom drinks too much, but she's not an alcoholic" or "My son parties a lot, and his grades have plummeted, but he says he's got it under control, and I believe him."

Common examples of rescues are pouring bottles down the sink, making excuses to others, keeping non-family members out of the home so they won't see alcoholic scenes, and cleaning up financial, legal, social, and medical messes that addicts are prone to make. All of these behaviors reflect the essence of rescue, offering something that you can't deliver; in this case, embodying the delusion that someone else can externally control an addict's use.

Examples of persecution are emotionally and/or physically abusing addicts to try to get them to change or to somehow balance the damage they cause by punishing them. The U.S. war on drugs continues to be a punishment-based enterprise that has resulted in the world's highest number of citizens behind bars and one of the least effective prevention programs of all western nations. Persecution and punishment tend to support addiction while clean boundaries tend to discourage it. Clean boundaries protect the boundary setter and influence the addict to face the consequences of their destructive behavior while realizing that addiction is a disease that requires understanding and treatment.

Heroin addicts are more likely to die of overdose; methamphetamine or cocaine dependence can result in psychotic symptoms; marijuana addiction is associated with amotivational syndrome in teenagers and dramatically increases their likelihood of using other drugs; and alcoholism causes (or amplifies) a number of physical ailments, many of which can be fatal.[2]

Families with addicted members tend to be closed systems. They resist revealing their needs to the outside world or allowing the outside world to participate in the family. Further, since the addict often refuses to consider recovery, the main channel the family needs to grow toward more mature and healthy relating is blocked, thus leaving the members to cycle endlessly between rigidity and chaos until the addiction is acknowledged and addressed.

Part of therapy with such systems is attuning to the members who are available (often not the addict) and helping them grow to the point that they are willing to break the unhealthy rules that they unconsciously have created to resist change.

What is addiction?

Addiction involves use of a euphoric substance that is progressive and/or out of control. "Progressive" refers to the fact that more of the substance is used over time. "Out of control" refers to the phenomenon of an addict being unable to say "no" to another dose under certain circumstances. For instance, children and adults suffering from attention deficit disorder often benefit from daily doses of amphetamine, but their use is not progressive. The same dose can have the desired focusing effect for years. Pursuing their "high," methamphetamine and cocaine addicts tend to use more quantity of drug, more frequently over time, and build up tolerance, thus requiring more drug to get their desired effect and prevent withdrawal. Ironically, since cocaine and amphetamine tend to use up available dopamine (an excitement neurotransmitter) in the brain, eventually addicts are often using primarily to avoid withdrawal, and can feel relatively little euphoric effects.

In this book I am distinguishing chemical dependence (addiction to drugs and/or alcohol) from other compulsive activities such as compulsive eating, sexual behavior, gambling, working, or exercise. There are similarities between chemical dependence and other compulsive activities (especially compulsive gambling), but there are a lot of differences too, and, in my opinion, treating these activities as if they are always completely analogous to chemical dependency can be trying to force a square peg into a round hole. That being said, if you believe you or a family member suffer from any form of compulsive disorder, it's a good idea to find a licensed therapist you trust and check it out.

How can I tell if someone in my family is chemically dependent?

This is sometimes a surprisingly difficult question. Lots of people drink or use drugs non-addictively. Much adolescent and young adult culture normalizes binge behavior. Almost every addict I've ever worked with initially maintained that they could control their use.

Key discriminators in discerning addiction are:

- Regular use to intoxication.

- Failed attempts to stop or control use.

- Unconscious lying about use. Addicts lie to themselves, and this leads to being unaware of lies to others.

- Deliberate lying about use. Addicts tend to rationalize lots of obvious destructive behaviors including deliberately lying to others.

- DUI's or other problems with the law.

- Damage to intimate relationships. Spouses and children of addicts tend to feel angry, concerned, powerless, frightened, or injured by the addict's use.

- Powerful relational taboos against discussing alcohol/drug use, exposing others to an intoxicated family member, or challenging destructive behaviors.

A striking characteristic of addiction is a profound self-centeredness in the user. Because chemically dependent individuals cause such suffering to others, even the most charming and charismatic addict will have an essential selfishness that becomes obvious when you explore their relationships. There is always a tension between the insistence on use of euphorics and the hurt and resentment of intimates resulting from such use.

Two couples I recently worked with provide examples of the contrast between substance use and abuse. One couple came in with a problem they were having with their twenty-year-old daughter. Even though both drank and occasionally smoked pot, neither felt injured or threatened by the other's use, both had high standards for all forms of self-regulation, and both experienced themselves and each other as successful, caring, and physically healthy. I've never found chemical dependence in a relationship like theirs.

A second couple, Jerry and Mandy, came in because Jerry insisted he could control his alcohol and drug use, and Mandy found this belief intolerable. Even though they agreed that his current consumption involved limited amounts (one or two drinks) only occasionally (once or twice a month), Jerry had a history of alcohol dependence and treatment as a young man, and recent failed attempts to quit entirely.

After intervention and treatment at age twenty, Jerry had been drug and alcohol free for ten years, a fact he referred to with pride as a sign that he could control his use. When I told him that years of abstinence were actually often a sign that an individual was prone to addiction, he shifted his rationalizations to his belief that he had "grown" in the intervening years and was now competent to control his drug and alcohol use.

Mandy, who had fallen in love with and married Jerry when he was sober, had been through two nightmare cycles of Jerry drinking (with some pot and cocaine use), followed by interventions with health care workers and failed attempts by Jerry to quit indefinitely. She was terrified of going through the nightmare again, but unconsciously avoided facing the fact that she was unwilling to set the only boundary she had left to influence Jerry to change: the boundary of refusing to live with him unless he was in recovery. Instead of setting this boundary, Mandy would complain, argue, and demean Jerry endlessly, while he responded with the same tired denials, rationalizations, and nasty counterattacks. They were the epitome of the popular definition of insanity: doing the same thing over and over again and expecting a different outcome. Both in their early forties, they had a nine-year-old son and twin five-year-old daughters. Typically, both tried to "protect" the children from Jerry's drug and alcohol use by conspiring to hide, lie, and rationalize. Mandy was horrified when I pointed out how this reflected her participation in their alcoholic system and was typical of the inevitable corruption that infects everyone who lives with an addict. The following is from their second session:

Mandy: "I found amphetamine in his briefcase, and I told him he had to leave."

Jerry: (Using a reasonable tone, with an "I'm cooperating, but she is *so* over-reacting" attitude.) "She told me to leave, so I did."

Keith: "Where are you staying?"

Mandy: "He's staying at the track. That's a message."

Jerry: "I'm not gambling that much. I like it because I enjoy being near the horses."

Keith: "You don't think there's a little 'screw you' to Mandy, staying at a place that famous for all kinds of out-of-control, destructive behaviors?"

Jerry: "I haven't lost any money, and I like the horses."

Mandy: "Just like you enjoy the 'taste' of margaritas."

Keith: "Good job telling Jerry to leave, Mandy. We talked about how you were resisting setting that boundary."

Mandy: "Yeah, great. Now what?"

Keith: "What do you both want?"

Jerry: "I want to be back with my family."

Mandy: "I want a sober husband."

Jerry: "If you would just lighten up …"

Mandy: "Lighten up? What, and say it's OK for you to use speed and drink?"

Jerry: "It was a mistake to get the speed. I won't do that again." (Mandy and I exchange a glance.)

Keith: "Well, here we are in a alcoholic system. Jerry, you're the alcoholic in denial. Mandy, you're being the persecutor trying to harass him into change, and I'm being recruited as the rescuer to offer goods I can't deliver."

Jerry: "What do you mean?"

Keith: "You deny that you are an addict. You want your family, you know that your use is intolerable to Mandy, but you want to live with her and use. Mandy hates your addiction but, until this week, has been unable to set the only boundary she had left to save her family: the boundary of refusing to live with you while you're not in recovery."

Jerry: "She should give me a chance to control my drinking. I haven't been drinking that much. I'm with her on meth and coke. I won't do those."

Keith: "How about pot?"

Jerry: "I don't see how pot once in a while hurts anybody. It's not that bad for you." (As Mandy begins a heated reply, I interrupt.)

Keith: "Let's be honest. Mandy, you're certain that Jerry's an alcoholic, and, if he uses anything, it is only a matter of time before it completely ruins your lives. I agree with you. Jerry, you disagree and think you should have *another* chance to try to use in a controlled way. Both of you hide all this from your children and most of your friends and family. Your solution for years has been increasing hostility towards each other, punctuated by periods of relatively little use, but always suspicion and contempt in the background. The only thing that's different this time is that Mandy told you to leave when she found the methamphetamine, and you, Jerry, are respecting her wishes." (Both nod reluctantly. This is an ugly picture that is obviously true to both of them. I continue.) "The main question today is, Mandy, are you willing to continue to set boundaries, and what are they?"

Mandy: "I've already kicked him out. What boundaries do I have left? I don't want a divorce."

Jerry: "Neither do I."

Keith: "What conditions do you have for Jerry coming home?"

Mandy: "What are my choices?"

Keith: "Since Jerry is currently respecting your boundaries, you have a number of choices. You could not allow him to come home unless he goes to one AA meeting a day for a week, or six months. You could insist on outpatient or inpatient alcohol/drug treatment, and/or drug testing. You could file for divorce, and if Jerry is not sober in recovery during the six-month interlocutory period, finalize it. You could stop lying about Jerry's use to your friends, family, and children."

Mandy: "I could never tell them that their father is an alcoholic."

Keith: "Why not? Don't you think Zack knows there's a problem and the twins feel it?" (Mandy nods reluctantly.)

Jerry: (All this talk is painful to him. He tries to pull us back into the addictive system.) "We should talk about it."

Keith: "Jerry, one characteristic of alcoholic systems is that, eventually, the coalcoholic is making unilateral decisions because she has lost trust for the addict. You can't talk effectively to someone you don't trust. Her kicking you out was the healthiest thing she's done in the last year. The very fact that you two have constellated this system tells me that you are an alcoholic. I know you love Mandy and the kids, and I'm trying to find a way you can be with them."

Mandy: "It's not fair that I have to make the decisions. He's the man, he should make the decisions."

Keith: "Addiction tends to ruin erotic polarity. The number one thing a feminine person needs in a masculine partner is for him to be trustable. Mandy, you have no trust for Jerry in this and many other areas. The number one thing a masculine person needs from a feminine person is support for his deepest purpose. Your deepest purpose, Jerry, is hopelessly obscured by the alcoholic system that you and Mandy have created. Mandy, of course it's not fair for you to have to make these unilateral decisions, but that's how addiction works. If you don't, you're surrendering to addiction. You've tried that for years."

Mandy: "OK. Get into treatment, and, if you're sober and in treatment for three weeks, you can come home."

Jerry: "Why can't I come home now? I miss the kids." (He tears up.)

Mandy: "I just don't feel safe."

This is typical of sessions with addicts and their spouses. There is lots of defensive enactment and very little attunement. Polarity is contaminated both by the fact that all chemical addictions ultimately interfere with libido, and masculine/feminine practice is always compromised by chemical dependency. As I explained to Jerry and Mandy, a feminine partner can't trust the integrity of a masculine addict because he will violate his principles to use. A masculine person can't trust the caring of a feminine addict because she will sacrifice love to use.

Addicts can't attune well because they are always lying to themselves about their addiction. Lying is a form of unexamined violence, and we've already explored in Chapter Six what unexamined violence can do to relationships. Attuning to an addict is painful, because you feel the distress of their lies and the taboos around directly addressing them. That's why the first steps in dealing with addiction are to wake up and get support.

Wake up and get support.

The first step of the Alcoholics Anonymous twelve step program is waking up to the fact that you have no control over your use[3]. In alanon and other programs for those close to addicts, the first step is waking up to the fact that you can't control your family member's alcohol/drug use. Breaking through denial is the hardest process in working with addicts and codependents. Jerry denied his drinking, and, to a certain extent, Mandy denied her contributions to the alcoholic system. Both eventually turned to me for support.

Getting support means sharing the truth with someone (and eventually many others) who is not surrendering to supporting the sick system, and who is able to attune to the suffering inherent in chemical dependence. AA and all related programs provide such attunement. Therapy of all forms helps, as does educating yourself and your family about what addiction is and how to deal with it.

The way to enter healthy states of consciousness and practice them when you have chemical dependence in your family is get support and learn how to discern between talking to someone you can attune to and trust, and talking to an addict in denial. This is especially important because, often, the only healthy options available for spouses are unilateral boundaries like the ones Mandy was setting for Jerry. Understandably, partners like Mandy feel deep resentment about having to unilaterally set boundaries for adults like Jerry who should be self-regulating.

Teen addicts.

When an addict is a teenager, parents will often feel resentment that, instead of relying on their child to proceed on the natural developmental path of progressively more effective self-regulation, they have to essentially treat their teen like a much younger child and set unilateral boundaries in the face of infantile outrage and protest. The following is the scene when Brian, the fifteen-year-old son of Rachel and Harry, was first informed he was to be escorted to Mountain View School because of his marijuana addiction and out-of-control behavior. He has just come home from the mall and walked into the living room of their house, where he encounters Rachel, Harry, and Leon, the six-and-a-half foot tall escort who has been hired to take Brian away:

Brian: "What's going on? Who's he?"

Leon: (He's the most relaxed person in the room. He's done this a hundred times, and he believes in his work.) "Hello, Brian, my name's Leon. I'm here to take you to Mountain View School in Idaho."

Brian: "No way." (He bolts for the door, but Leon glides in front of him, blocking his exit.) "You can't do this."

Harry: "I'm sorry son. We have to do our best to help you, and you don't realize you need help. You're addicted to pot and God knows what else, and you're out of control." (Rachel now is crying so hard she can barely talk.)

Brian: "Mom! Don't let them do this."

Rachel: "We've packed your bags. They're in Leon's rental car. You can't take your computer stuff or your phone."

Brian: "I'll do what you say. I'll stop smoking pot. I won't ditch school. Don't send me away."

Harry: "We're sorry son, you have to go."

Brian: "I hate you! I hate both of you! You are so full of shit."

Leon: "Time to go, Brian. We can do it quietly, or I'll have to restrain you."

Brian: "Get away from me."

Leon: (Take's Brian gently by the arm.) "Let's go. Say goodbye to your mom and dad. The people at the school will tell you when you can talk to them again." (He escorts Brian from the room while Harry and Rachel hold each other.)

Rachel and Harry are lucky enough to be able to afford a special school. Most parents aren't and need to get help from county and state resources, and the recovery community. The following is from a marriage counseling session they had two weeks later:

Keith: "How has it been without Brian in the house?" (Rachel and Harry exchange a guilty look.)

Harry: "I miss him, but it's been a relief to not have him around. We've hardly fought at all. Albert and Hannah miss him, but they've been more affectionate and relaxed also."

Rachel: "I'm not worried every night. We get updates from his counselor at the school, and they say we can talk to him soon if he keeps working his program."

Keith: "Sounds like he's doing well."

Harry: "His counselor says he's cooperating and beginning to get what kind of risks he's been running the last two years."

Keith: "What's different in your relationship?"

Rachel: "I'm remembering how much I love Harry." (Harry smiles, a little embarrassed.)

Harry: "It's easier to be patient with Albert and Hannah with Brian not home in the evenings. I wasn't aware of how much tension I had about his safety. It seems that the more patient I am with the kids, the more Rachel likes me."

Keith: "Maybe you two are rediscovering your love affair. That's always been there at the heart of your relationship."

We all need each other. We all need support. Support, like everything else, is harder when there is an addict in the family, but it is even more important to insist on it when there is an addict in the family. As we attune with ourselves and trusted others, and learn how to discern healthy and unhealthy perspectives, impulses, and behaviors, it frees us up to gradually learn how to attune to our spouse, child, sibling, or parent in recovery. Not only Harry and Rachel, but also Albert and Hannah needed support for understanding Brian's addiction and self-destructive habits, and how they needed to grow through the injuries their family had endured dealing with these things. Here is some conversation they had at the dinner table that night:

Rachel: "Albert and Hannah, how has it been for you with Brian not here?"

Albert: "There's less fighting."

Hannah: "Brian used to tickle me. Why did he have to go?"

Rachel: "He was addicted to pot, and he kept doing dangerous things, even when we told him not to."

Albert: "What do you mean 'addicted.' Isn't anybody that smokes pot addicted."

Harry: (*"What did Keith say?"*) "There are three kinds of people, son. Some people can drink or use drugs and never have a problem. Your mom is like that. She can make one beer last a month." (He laughs, but then notices nobody else is laughing, and quickly moves on.) "Some people can drink or use drugs if they have rules for controlling their use and can follow those rules. I rarely have more than two beers when I drink, and I regret it when I have more. Some people, when they use drugs or alcohol, can't follow any rules. They use more and more, and sometimes they just can't say 'no.' That's addiction. Brian just couldn't say 'no' to pot, so he had to stop using it. He couldn't do it by himself and didn't realize how dangerous his life was, so we had to send him to Mountain View School so they could help him."

Hannah: "Am I addicted?" (The others laugh.)

Harry: "No, sweetheart. But when you get older, if you try drugs or alcohol, you'll find out what kind of person you are. You might drink rarely and not need rules, like Mommy, you might need rules, like me, or you might not be able to use in a controlled way at all, like Brian."

Albert: "I don't want to drink or use pot. The kids who do are losers."

Rachel: "Not all of them, Albert. Lots of people in this country drink or use drugs and are not addicts. The safest way to go, of course, is to not use at all. It would be a relief to me if neither of you every used drugs or alcohol."

Harry: "Me too. I've been so worried about Brian. I feel a lot safer that he's in a special school that will help him." (There is a warm, caring feeling around the table. The family is in community, discussing important issues and loving Brian.)

1. McGoey (2006)

2. *Ibid*

3. Wilson (1939)

12

Therapy and Attunement

I love psychotherapy. I decided to become a therapist in 1965, was first licensed in 1975, and have been busy ever since studying and practicing different systems of therapy. There is a magic in therapy that is most purely reflected in Carl Rogers' work, where he and his students demonstrated that simply being in a therapeutic relationship where the helper is empathetic, congruent, transparent, self-disclosing, and caring results in growth and enhanced well-being in the client.[1]

One explanation of this effect can be found in current research, which demonstrates the presence of mirror neurons in our brain that can reflect *the state of consciousness* of someone we're relating to. If I am in the presence of a person who is relentlessly empathetic, congruent, and caring, even in the face of my defensive states, my brain will reflexively mirror those qualities to some extent. Since we tend to construct internal working models of important relationships, with enough practice I will be more likely to unilaterally bring empathy, congruence, and caring to bear on my defensive states; in other words, to self-attune.

When we can bring insight and empathy online simultaneously we are practicing what Dan Siegal calls "mindsight."[2] Neuroscience has demonstrated mindsight to be associated with neural integration, a central feature of mental health that we will explore in more detail in Chapter Fourteen.

There are many definitions of therapy. Every therapist has his or her favorites, and the two I offer in my first book, *Waking Up,* are:

- Cultivating compassion and depth of consciousness to support healthy perspectives and actions.

- Co-creating a culture in which the client and the client's universe are cherished, each moment is experienced as a gift and an opportunity, and healthy perspectives and actions are considered beautiful, good, and true.

In that book I go on to say that the process of therapy is the clinician offering various combinations of relating, teaching, inspiring, confronting, interpreting, and directing, with the purpose of remediating symptoms, enhancing health, and supporting development.[3]

In the context of this book, therapy can be described as a particular form of mutual attunement, where the therapist takes on the responsibility to attune to self and client with the goal of helping the client in every way possible within the legal and ethical confines of the therapeutic relationship.

A peculiar quality of psychotherapy is that, even though it is complementary as is all communication (sender and receiver must cooperate for communication to occur), it is asymmetrical in that the therapist has different responsibilities and functions from the client. It is the therapist's job to attune to self and client and to provide professionalism, safety, and maintain the therapeutic relationship. It is the client's job to discern whether they are being adequately served and to hold up their end of the contract (show up, pay their bill, give advance notice of cancellations, make an effort to improve, and risk honest communication as an intrapersonal and interpersonal standard).

There are many such asymmetrical relationships in our lives. Parent/child, teacher/student, doctor/patient, and employer/employee are all examples; each has its own constellation of responsibilities and boundaries. It's the parent's or professional's job to know the responsibilities and boundaries of their work and be true to them to the best of their ability; this is what distinguishes these relationships from friendships and casual acquaintances.

When does therapy help?

Good therapy always helps. Sitting down with a competent, caring, knowledgeable person with the intent of better understanding yourself and others and to function more optimally in all the environments of your life is going to be helpful. Sure, there are bad therapists. Everybody in the business has had some personal experience with a colleague who collapsed and didn't optimally or responsibly serve a client. Therapists seem to be frequent targets in TV, film, and literature, and it is easy to caricature a profession where the main product is earnest, authentic, intimate relating. Mostly, though, therapists are well-trained, caring professionals who bring their best selves to the work and are dedicated to helping clients.

Simply the decision to seek therapy represents intent to improve, grow, and change for the better, thus reinforcing neural networks associated with positive intent. Often my clients feel significantly better after just scheduling a session.

When should I see a therapist?

When you have difficulty improving your ability to attune to yourself or any important intimate, therapy is usually a good idea. Individual attunement (attending to my emotions, thoughts, and impulses with the intent to do right) and interpersonal attunement (adding attention to another's emotions, thoughts, and impulses) are integrative processes that tend to improve with practice and feedback. Therapy is a place where training in, practice of, and feedback about attunement routinely takes place.

If we hit a spot where we can't seem to improve but instead create repetitive negative dramas, we are often being influenced by defensive states that are hard to perceive. Therapy can direct caring attention toward such blind spots to help us first differentiate the parts of us that resist change and then integrate them into a larger whole. This differentiation/integration process is a natural developmental outcome of our innate drive to create meaning and our need for more complex, inclusive, wider understanding as we expand our knowledge and wisdom. The "include and transcend" rhythm of human development that we've explored in previous chapters is characterized by this drive to expand awareness, leading to differentiation, leading to integration, leading to expanded awareness, and so on.

In the following session with Jim (whom we met with his wife, Sally, and sons, Jake and Eric, in the beginning of this book), he has encountered a block to his ability to attune with Jake, his older son. At this time Jake is thirteen, in the seventh grade, and is entering a stage where he is sometimes defiant and contemptuous of adults. His brother, nine-year-old Eric, is a happy, compliant fourth grader whose position in the family has been to try to do right and treat everybody with care and respect (thus avoiding most conflicts and encouraging satisfying relating at home and school). Jim clashes with Jake and then fights with Sally about his parenting style. Having benefited from therapy episodically over the last ten years, Jim, at Sally's urging, called me for a session:

Jim: "Jake drives me crazy."

Keith: "What do you mean?"

Jim: "He knows what sets me off, and he does it again and again. Then I try to discipline him, and Sally gets on *my* case."

Keith: "That feels unfair to you."

Jim: "You're damn right it feels unfair. She wants me to be an involved father, and here I am trying to teach Jake decent values and she gets pissed at me. It doesn't make sense."

In attachment research, the main discriminating characteristic of adults with secure attachment styles is that they *had made sense, or were in the process of making sense,* of their lives.[4] A huge part of therapy is helping clients engage in the compassionate self-reflection necessary to first differentiate aspects which resist understanding and change, and then integrate those parts into a "larger" self. This is what creates coherent narratives.

Jim is a more masculine person who deals with life from a predominantly rational worldview. Thus, his understanding needs to be consistent with his masculine predispositions (problems need to be identified and solved, opponents need to be defeated, and justice needs to be served) and his rational worldview (perspectives and techniques need to be supported by observable, scientific data).

Keith: "It makes sense to me."

Jim: "What do you mean?"

Keith: "We've encountered this countless times in your work over the last ten years. What's the mistake you are most prone to making with Sally and the kids, and especially Jake?"

Jim: "To make content more important than how I'm presenting it."

Keith: "Bull's-eye! How is that happening with Jake and Sally?"

Jim: "I get so frustrated with Jake making the same mistakes, and using his snotty tone, that I just lose it."

Keith: "What do you lose?"

Jim: (This question is confusing because it directs him right to the heart of his defensive structure, the neurological network he constellated as an infant in response to his demeaning mother, which can be activated when he's challenged in certain ways. Therapists use confusion as a road sign to direct them into conflict areas. Jim, safe enough with me to explore his confusion, answers slowly, reaching for what feels true.) "I get so disgusted that I lose my ability to be kind."

Keith: "What has *always been* Sally's reaction when you are unkind to her or the kids?"

Jim: (He laughs, a signal that, at this moment, he has differentiated his contemptuous defense and integrated it into a larger self.) "She always hates it and gets in my face."

Keith: (He's a masculine person, so I want him to commit to a solution. Commitments, deals, and contracts are often sacred to masculine people.) "So, you tell me the solution to this problem."

Jim: "I need to be kind when I talk to Jake. That's easier said than done."

Keith: "When you were small, who was snotty to you?"

Jim: "You know. My Mom could hit, and scream and make me feel worthless. I know now she couldn't help it, but, man, I hated it when I was growing up. And my Dad just let her. I despised how weak he was."

Keith: "Not like Sally."

Jim: (Laughing again.) "No, she insists on good tones, and I admire her for that. Though, you know, she lets Jake get away with being snotty to her. It doesn't make sense."

Keith: "Doesn't it? Do you think her distress over your anger, not to mention her own family experiences, might be influencing her with Jake, as well as you?"

Jim: "She thinks it's all me."

Keith: "As long as you use unkind tones, she'll have an excuse to not look at her part. Why don't you set yourself the standard of zero tolerance for emotional violence, including unkind tones? Do your best to relate as kindly and patiently as you can, and then come in with Sally for a conjoint session. I suggest you tell her everything we've discussed and invite her to come in together in two weeks."

Jim: (The masculine grows best in the presence of loving challenge.) "I'll do that."

Two weeks later Sally and Jim come in together for a conjoint session. Since Jim has had more awareness of his defensive tendencies and more understanding that, to a certain extent, Jake and Sally have been paying the price for the injuries he experienced as a child, his extreme angry reactions and impulses to demean make more sense to him, and his strong commitment to justice has strengthened his resolve to use kind tones "come hell or high water" (his words). As he makes more sense of his life, he has more flexibility of response in stressful situations. Increased response flexibility is another characteristic of attunement and coherent life narrative:[5]

Keith: "How have things been the last two weeks?"

Sally: "Wonderful. Jim's been so patient with the kids. Jake's responding, too. He's talking more with Jim, and they've been playing basketball every evening."

Jake: "He's getting too good. He's beating me sometimes."

Keith: "Let me tell you, he'll get better and better. I don't like to lose but, I've got to say, I was proud of my son when he beat me in tennis for the first time."

Jake: "I am proud of him. He works on his game."

Keith: "How has it been with you two?"

Jake: "We've been more connected." (Sally agrees.)

Keith: "Sally, Jim mentioned that Jake sometimes is disrespectful of you." (She nods.) "What's that like for you?"

Sally: "He's just a kid. I cut him some slack."

Jim: "You let him be rude too much."

Sally: "That's because you're mean to him so much."

Keith: "Sally, what's valid about what Jim said?"

Sally: "What did he say?"

Keith: (When someone loses her ability to hear, it's usually a sign of a defensive state.) "Jim said that you let Jake be rude too much. What's valid about that?"

Sally: "Jake can get nasty, but he's just a kid."

Jim: "He's thirteen years old."

Sally: "You just want him to be perfect."

Keith: "What's happening right now?"

Jim: "It's the same old fight."

Keith: "Do you notice how it started?"

Sally: "I admitted Jake can be nasty, and Jim jumped all over me, like he always does."

Keith: "You admitted Jake can be nasty, and then you made an excuse for him. You said 'He's just a kid.'"

Sally: "OK. I admit that I defend him. Jim's too harsh."

Keith: "How has he been the last two weeks?"

Sally: "I already said, he's been great."

Keith: "So, what should he do if he thinks you are letting Jake be rude in a way that doesn't support Jake's development?"

Sally: "He could tell me nicely."

Jim: (Grunting sarcastically.) "Huh. As if that would make any difference. You never listen to me when I tell you he's being inappropriate."

Keith: "Jim, what happened to being kind, come Hell or high water."

Jim: (Looking embarrassed.) "You're right. I'm sorry, Sally. I just get so frustrated because I don't think it's good for him or you."

Sally: (Impressed at Jim's recovery. This is response flexibility at work. She's not used to this kind of self-regulation, and it disarms her, makes her feel safe, and enables her to go deeper into self-reflection.) "Well, you're right too. I can't remember when I really listened to you when you told me you thought Jake was being rude. I've always had to defend him."

Keith: "Sally, do you believe that Jim can self-regulate when he's frustrated and use kind tones when he intervenes between you and Jake?"

Sally: "I don't know; I'll have to see what it's like."

Keith: "Jim, I suggest that when you think Jake is being rude to Sally, you tell her respectfully what you think serves everybody's best interests and then accept whatever she decides to do. Feminine partners like direction. They want to hear what you think is in the highest good. They hate coercion, where they believe they will be punished if they don't comply."

Jim: "Sure, I've been trying to do that anyway."

Keith: "How about you, Sally? Are you willing to feel into yourself, feel into Jim, and consider what's valid if he gives you this kind of feedback?"

Sally: "As long as he's not mean to me if I don't agree." (Jim finds this reasonable.)

Keith: "I suggest you go home, practice this for a couple of weeks, and then come in with the kids for a family session."

Next session, all four come in and sit down. We've occasionally had family sessions in the past, but none in the last two years or so. Jake, going through the dramatic physical and neurological changes of adolescence, is strikingly more mature physically, cognitively, and emotionally. Eric, finally leaving his status as clueless youngest child and feeling the power of being an academically and athletically successful fourth grader, is more self-aware and assertive.

Good parenting is a process that supports development and growth in everyone. Techniques that work for younger children can leave older children nonplussed, and vice versa, so parents are regularly being challenged to grow in response to their developing children. In general, the arc of change in healthy families tends to be the more responsibility the child demonstrates, the more adult credibility they are allowed by parents.

Keith: "Wow. You boys are growing up. Your parents tell me you are in the seventh and fourth grades." (The boys nod.) "Have things been any different the last two weeks?"

Jake: "I don't know."

Eric: "Me neither."

Keith: (This is a common response with kids. I asked them first because I want them to know that their opinions are valuable and will be elicited in this session. Children have a strong sense of personal dignity. This is where Jake and Jim have been butting heads. Jake has learned to sometimes stand up for his personal dignity the same way his father instinctively does: by attacking people who threaten him.) "Well, parents, what's been different and the same?"

Jim: "I tried telling Sally when she was putting up with too much, and it worked a couple of times."

Sally: "It was harder to let Jim interrupt than I thought, but he was trying to be nice; I've got to give him that."

Keith: "Did you feel supported by his feedback?"

Sally: "Well, I didn't let Jake have a sleepover on a school day."

Jake: "It's the NBA playoffs, Mom. Justin's dad has wide screen plasma TV. You don't understand."

Sally: "I let you stay over Friday, right?"

Jake: "Yeah."

Keith: "Jake, was your dad different when you and your mom were talking about the school day sleepover?"

Jake: "He wasn't such an ass."

Jim: (Threateningly.) "Jake!"

Sally: (Concerned.) "Jake."

Keith: "Wow, Jake, that got quite a reaction. How does it feel in your body when you call your father an 'ass.'"

Jake: (The masculine, concerned with justice, is a natural lawyer.) "I didn't call him an ass, I said he wasn't such an ass." (Eric laughs at the forbidden word being thrown around so indiscriminately.)

Keith: "Good point, but you know it's a taboo word that will make your dad mad. Right?"

Jake: "I guess."

Keith: "Does it feel good, bad, or neutral to say forbidden words?

Jake: "I don't know. It doesn't feel good."

Keith: "Why do you think you used it, then?"

Jake: "I don't know."

Keith: "Do you want to use words that make your parents mad?"

Jake: "No."

Keith: "So, they must just slip out. How would you like them to correct you? What would be a respectful way your father could tell you that it's against family rules to refer to someone as an 'ass'?"

Jake: "He could just say that; it's against the rules."

Jim: (Frustrated.) "I do that all the time. You ..."

Keith: (Modeling for the boys how to confront their Dad respectfully.) "No offense, Jim, but that's not a kind tone, and I thought your new standard was zero tolerance for emotional violence."

Jim: (To the boys' obvious surprise, he apologizes.) "I'm sorry, Jake. Keith's right, I don't ever want to be disrespectful, even when I think you are. I would appreciate it if you wouldn't use the word with the family."

Jake: "Sure, Dad. No big deal."

Keith: "Look at Sally, you guys. What do you think she's feeling?" (Jim, Jake, and Eric look over at Sally, who's beaming.)

Eric: "She's happy."

Keith: "Why do you think she's happy?"

Eric: "She likes it when we're nice to each other."

Keith: "You notice how you can be respectful, even when you're mad?" (They all nod.) "I suggest that you have a new family rule, 'We're always respectful, even if we're mad.'"

Sally: "I like that rule."

Keith: "Are you willing to let Jim help you with the boys? They're growing up fast, but they're still kids, and they'll forget once in awhile."

Sally: "As long as he uses a good tone."

Keith: (Challenging Jim.) "Well, Jim, the pressure's on to be kind."

Jim: (He laughs confidently; this has been a validating session for him, and he likes the idea of the new rule.) "I think I can handle it, but if I can't, I think these guys will let me know." (The kids laugh.)

Keith: "Remember, boys, as long as you use a respectful tone, and accept that your parents have the last word, you can say just about anything. That's a pretty cool thing to be able to do in a family." (Everybody smiles, and Sally glows. These kinds of intimate dialogs are among her favorite moments and often when she finds Jim the most attractive.)

Therapy sessions are like snowflakes: No two sessions are exactly the same, but they all share certain basic characteristics. There are clients who desire to grow, therapists who desire to help, and healing relationships that it is the therapist's responsibility to establish and maintain.

There are dozens of systems of therapy, all effective in certain circumstances. I spent thirty years studying martial arts and found that the more highly skilled and widely experienced the practitioner, the more appreciation and identification he or she felt for other systems. I've found the same phenomenon to be true for systems of therapy. My first book, *Waking Up*, synthesized many approaches, all of which I've found to be beautiful, good, and true.

How to choose a therapist.

Ask your friends or relatives if they have had positive experiences with licensed practitioners. These therapists are good candidates for you. Talk to these candidates on the phone, and ask them about their training, experience, and personal life. For instance, you probably want a therapist who is a parent to work with you on parenting, or a therapist who has a successful marriage to work with you on your marriage. If you like them on the phone and feel that they can help you, schedule an appointment.

During your first appointment you can mutually attune with your therapist and discuss what you're feeling. Good therapists do not get defensive when challenged and offer opinions about what they think is in your best interests. If you feel "felt" by this person, comfortable with them, and have a sense that they can help you grow, it's a good sign to continue.

If you become uncomfortable in any way during a session and your therapist doesn't notice, bring it to his or her attention. How a therapist deals with such challenges is revealing. If you feel more safe and known after your discussion, it is a good sign. If you continue to feel less safe and known after repeated discussions, it can be a bad sign and sometimes a signal to change therapists. Good therapists will make it easy for you to transition to another practitioner, and support you being true to your inner voices.

Feeling into yourself and considering what serves the highest good, and feeling into others and considering what serves the highest good are integrative processes that support individual and relational development. A therapy session is an environment that examines, supports, and facilitates our ongoing abilities to attune to ourselves and others.

1. Gilliland (1998)

2. Siegal (2005)

3. Witt (2005)

4. Siegal (2005)

5. *Ibid*

13

Attunement is Spiritual Practice

The following session with Harry and Rachel's family is typical of the later stages of therapy, when family members are more self-aware, self-reflective, accepting of different members' various worldviews, and the family standard is to support openness, growth, honesty, and repair. Issues in such sessions tend to be less about problems and more about transformation. This is consistent with Ken Wilber's observation that the further we grow on any developmental line, the more spiritual that line feels.[1] At this point, Brian is seventeen, Albert is eleven, and Hannah is seven. The session begins with Rachel, who sings in the church choir, being distressed that Harry won't go to services with her and the kids:

Rachel: "I love going to church, and I wish you'd go, Harry."

Harry: "Rachel, I just don't believe in that stuff."

Rachel: "I don't want to be married to an atheist."

Hannah: "What's an atheist?"

Rachel: "An atheist is someone who doesn't believe in God."

Harry: "Rachel, I hate it when you do this. I've told you, it's not as if I don't believe in God. I just don't believe in Noah, Adam and Eve, and Jesus being the son of God, and all the Bible stories."

Brian: "You're going to Hell, Dad." (Albert laughs.)

Rachel: "I don't believe in Hell. I'm not a fire-and-brimstone fundamentalist, I'm just a Christian."

Keith: "Do you believe in Hell, Brian?"

Brian: "I guess not. I don't think it's right for people to suffer forever just because they aren't Christians."

Keith: "Do you believe in some kind of God or infinite spirit, Harry?"

Harry: "That's more what I think; that there's some kind of infinite spirit that we can't understand that's everywhere."

Keith: "How do you experience it?"

Harry: "In nature. Believe it or not, I'll often feel it on the golf course." (The family laughs.)

Rachel: "Come on Harry; next you'll say you feel God at the Sports Bar." (This completely cracks up Brian and Alpert, and Brian starts doing a riff on God at the Sports Bar.)

Brian: "I can see it, Dad. The Lakers are down by five with three seconds to go. Suddenly, Koby makes a three, steals the inbound pass, launches it across the court, and swish, another three. It's a miracle from God! Then, your stingy friend David buys a round for everyone. Another miracle!" (Harry looks distressed as his family laughs at him.)

Keith: "Come on, you guys. Your dad said he feels connected to spirit in nature. Maybe you could get off his case and ask him about it."

Rachel: (A little embarrassed, she turns to Harry.) "OK, tell us what you mean."

Harry: (Now he's embarrassed, but he answers as best he can.) "Sometimes when I'm in a beautiful place, I feel like I'm part of something larger than me. It's like all of nature is one thing, and we're all part of it. Sometimes it seems like beneath nature, or inside or all around nature, there's something larger like God." (This brings a respectful silence to the family. It's the first time that Harry has tried to articulate his personal experience of spirituality.)

Keith: "Feeling absorbed in, or one with, nature is called nature mysticism.[2] Have any of you felt that deep sense of the sacred; of expanding larger than your body?"

Brian: "You know, they taught us how to meditate at Mountain View. When I'd done it for a couple of months, sometimes I would feel like I was floating in space; except I was the space."

Keith: "Spiritual traditions say that feeling one with nature is nature mysticism. If you feel deeper into nature and sense a transcendent presence, or God, they call it deity mysticism.[3] Feeling Christ in your heart is deity mysticism. That's what you feel in church, Rachel. If you feel one with pure emptiness or void, as meditators do, one name for it is formless mysticism.[4] They all are good. They all make us deeper and healthier. What do you think of all this, Hannah?"

Hannah: (At seven, this mostly passes her by, but Hannah's opinion is honored by the family.) "I like to go to church with Mommy. I like the singing and my Sunday dress."

Keith: "Spoken like a true feminine person. You like spirituality in communion with others, and pleasure in sound and texture. Masculine people tend to find spirituality in solitude and emptiness."[5]

Rachel: "I still want Harry to come to church with us. What kind of message does it send to the kids; you off playing golf on Sunday?"

Brian: "I agree with Dad. I don't believe Jesus rose from the dead, or any of that stuff. That's superstition."

Keith: "How about you, Albert? What's your opinion? Your brother has meditated and felt one with emptiness. Your father sometimes feels one with nature, and even deeper to some unknowable presence that is deeper than nature. Your mother feels a sense of the sacred in church, singing with the choir, and can feel Christ in her heart."

Albert: "I think it's dumb that they argue about it."

Keith: "What do you mean?"

Albert: "Just because you think something different, it doesn't mean it's wrong. That's what my parents say, and then they do it with this church stuff. Sunday services are OK, but sometimes I'm bored. I don't know."

Keith: "People with different worldviews do tend to argue with each other. Research has shown us is that, when people keep growing and developing, they end up like Albert, with a felt sense of appreciation for all points of view.[6] When we feel into ourselves and others, we tend to cultivate this integral understanding. Clare Graves and Ken Wilber call this the Integral level of development."[7]

Oneness with nature is nature mysticism. Oneness with a supreme being, or God, is deity mysticism. Oneness with emptiness is formless mysticism. Oneness with the world and emptiness, both solitary and communing with everything, is non-dual awareness.[8] Oneness in partners loving each other is tantric practice. They're all good. They all involve attunement.

Spiritual practice, practices that cultivate the above experiences, tend to support more compassion, more caring, and more awareness; all qualities that are central to attunement. They all support health and development. They are all beautiful, good, and true.

Five days after the above session, eleven-year-old Albert has happily played in the pool all afternoon and is lying, watching the sky, on the front lawn. It's 5:30 on a summer night, and the clouds are luminescent. He feels like he's falling into the clouds and is one with the clouds. It is an intensely blissful experience that he has drifted into by chance. Children can be enormously powerful hypnotic subjects, capable of entering intense altered states, and Albert is allowing his consciousness to extend into the clouds. He doesn't hear his father calling him to dinner. Finally, Harry walks out the front door and, thinking Albert has been ignoring his calls, is about to yell angrily at him. Just in time, he tries to hold onto his anger and feel into Albert. Harry senses a state of spiritual oneness and is instantly soothed. *"This is what Keith meant by nature mysticism. He's completely absorbed."*

Harry looks up where his son's eyes are and sees the beautiful pink clouds, and he feels oneness. Even slightly mirroring a transcendent state conveys a warm sense of the sacred. This experience is a form of what spiritual teachers call transmission.[9] Albert spontaneously entered a state of nature mysticism, oneness with nature, and Harry, attuning to him, received a transmission and entered a similar state.

That night, Rachel is rehearsing with the church choir. They are just perfecting a new song, *Heal the world through me Lord,* are completely dialed in and lost in the music. Rachel feels herself consumed in the joy of devotional surrender and has a delicious sense of Christ's love flowing through her into the world. Other members of the choir are having similar experiences, and the singing becomes more passionate and fervent. The choir members feel their own joy and worship, feel it in each other, and the energy amplifies and becomes more intense and celebratory. Their oneness with Christ recapitulates a Deity mysticism experience that is as old as human consciousness. As they finish, Rachel is reminded of the therapy session. *"I guess Harry feels something like this in nature. I love him so much."*

Ken Wilber, one of my favorite writers and teachers, defines spirituality in a number of ways. Since spirituality is such a wide, important, and omnipresent aspect of human relating, interfacing with most of our experience and subtly influencing much of our decision making, I wholeheartedly support the idea that it is best examined from multiple perspectives. He maintains that spirituality can be viewed variously as:

- A quality of experience we can inhabit by design or circumstance at any stage of development.
- A characteristic of the highest levels on most developmental lines.
- A line of development itself.[10]

Formless Mysticism.

There were a number of good reasons that the instructors at Mountain View taught Brian how to meditate. Studies show that people don't deepen significantly on the self, cognitive, moral, or values lines between twenty-five and fifty-five, with one exception. Skip Alexander conducted studies on transcendental meditation that showed a deepening of two developmental levels on these lines after four years of daily meditative practice.[11]

For the past twenty-eight years, before I go to work to do therapy, teach, study, or write, I've meditated. My meditations have changed as I've changed, but certain things have remained very much the same. At a certain point in the process, I feel a oneness with pure emptiness.

Spiritual practitioners have been trying to describe this experience for twenty-five hundred years, and I doubt if any of them has ever been completely satisfied with their explanations. As Ken Wilber says in *Kosmic Consciousness*, "It's not a thing, it's an atmosphere."[12] Language is linear and dual in nature, and emptiness is an experience like the taste of chocolate. Could there be any description of chocolate that would result in you knowing the taste, texture, and feel of chocolate? I doubt it. You would have to take a bite of chocolate and see for yourself. Meditation provides the tools to explore the experience of emptiness.

Self-attunement involves feeling into your sensations, emotions, thoughts, and impulses with the intent serve the highest good. If your intent is spiritual practice, the highest good is often served by entering a state where you feel one with a vast, formless void. One way of experiencing this state is witness meditation. If you want to try it, you can do the following exercise:

Sitting comfortably, take eight deep, relaxed breaths. Observe your sensations, but recognize that you are not your sensations. You are a deeper witness that is larger than your sensations and observes without identifying with them.

What emotions are you feeling? Whether you are happy, sad, euphoric, or depressed, you do not equal any of these feelings. You are a deeper witness that is larger than your emotions and observes them as they ebb and flow.

What thoughts and impulses are you experiencing? Observe how they enter and exit your consciousness. You are a deeper witness who is larger than your thoughts and impulses, who can observe them as they enter and leave your consciousness but who does not identify with any of them.

Relax into this witness that observes all objects (the world, your body, your senses, feelings, thoughts, and impulses) but is not itself an object. As you engage in this practice, you will eventually begin to feel a vast peace come over you and a sense of being one with all things, which are always arising out of emptiness and returning to emptiness. The more you practice witness meditation, the more you tend to feel one with emptiness or the fertile void. Some spiritual traditions define this as formless mysticism.

Shared spiritual practice.

Rachel and Harry scheduled the following conjoint therapy session after they had a fight about sex. Rachel told Harry that she wanted "more connection" during lovemaking, and Harry took offense:

Harry: "I'm tired of having to jump through hoops all the time. Can't we just make love and not talk it to death?"

Rachel: "I need to feel connected to make love. You always close your eyes, and you seem somewhere else." (Harry shifts in his chair and looks out the window.)

Keith: "Harry, you look a little uncomfortable as Rachel talks. What's up?"

Harry: "Sure, so I close my eyes. What's the big deal?"

Keith: "First of all, let's remember that we're talking about erotic attunement. The biggest problem with sexual issues in general are critical judgments we make about ourselves and others."

Rachel: "I'm not making any judgments. I just want to feel connected."

Keith: "You're both making all kinds of critical judgments. You're critical of Harry for closing his eyes and not being connected enough. Harry, you're critical of Rachel for wanting to talk stuff to death and for not being fully satisfied with your lovemaking. I suggest you feel into your selves and each other and reach for what's valid about the other person's experience and yearning."

Harry: "I know it's good to be connected; sometimes I just don't know how to do it."

Rachel: "It's fine to just have easy sex sometimes, and I enjoy making love with Harry. I don't know what to do either when I want more connection."

Keith: "Do you practice the breathing exercises I showed you; breathe down the front and up the back alone, and then together, holding each other?"

Harry: "I forgot. And, you know, I liked doing the breathing alone and with Rachel."

Keith: "You might want to start again." (They both nod.) "What do you think of when you make love?" (Again, Harry looks uncomfortable.)

Keith: "Come on Harry, what is it?"

Harry: "Sometimes I fantasize Rachel making love with another woman, or me making love to her from behind; like doggy style." (He looks away from Rachel as he speaks.)

Keith: "Look at Rachel right now." (Harry looks her in the eye, and she looks interested. This clearly surprises him.) "Rachel, maybe you could tell Harry your reactions."

Rachel: "I think it's sweet that you're fantasizing about me. Why haven't you ever asked that we do that position?"

Harry: "You said it was demeaning to women." (Rachel looks confused.) "You know, when we saw that French film?"

Rachel: "Harry, he was cheating on his wife and treating her horribly. It wasn't the position. Besides, we saw that movie two years ago. You mean all this time you've assumed that I don't like doggy style?" (Harry nods.) "That's ridiculous." (Harry looks away.)

Keith: "Rachel, Harry finally gets it together to share something he's been keeping from you for two years, and you call him ridiculous. I don't think that encourages openness."

Rachel: "I'm sorry, sweetheart. I actually like that position sometimes." (Harry smiles at her.)

Keith: "Now you're connecting; telling each other what you like and don't like without critical judgment. Feeling into yourself *without critical judgment* and feeling into your partner *without critical judgment,* supports polarity. We've talked about polarity in other sessions."

Harry: "I do try to access my humor and my dark side when we make love."

Rachel: "We've had better sex this year than I can remember."

Harry: "Then why did you want to have this session? Why aren't you satisfied?" (Rachel and I look at each other and start laughing. After two beats, Harry joins us.) "OK. I remember. The feminine is never satisfied for long and is always wanting to find ways of creating more love."

Keith: "Yes! Look at Rachel as you talk." (Harry looks at her smiling fondly at him and relaxes.) "I suggest you go home and start telling each other what you like, want, are scared of, and fantasize about. If either of you starts making a critical judgment about anything, the other has to tickle them till they stop." (Both laugh.) "This is a form of tantric practice; of shared spiritual practice. As you learn to courageously evoke pleasure in your partner, and offer your partner your vulnerability and pleasure, erotic polarity tends to be enhanced, and you are literally making more love."

It's three months later, and Rachel and Harry are making love. It's Sunday afternoon, and the kids have gone to Disneyland with Rachel's parents, and they feel like they have all the time in the world. Harry feels into his heart, Rachel's heart, and the rhythm of lovemaking, and offers gentle direction into opening Rachel to increasing levels of pleasure. He's learned what opens and closes her, and how to read her signals. Rachel feels his love and enjoyment, and surrenders more deeply into her pleasure, feeling her heart open in devotional love to Harry as he enters her, caresses her, and receives her caresses. She allows her experience to flow outward into sound, movement, and breath. Gradually their rhythms harmonize and their pleasure increases, level upon level, until they both become lost in orgasm. As this happens they feel no distinction between themselves, their bodies, emptiness, or the world. Everything is, was, and will be at this perfect instant. They are lost in a non-dual, tantric moment.

Spiritual practices tend to go in two different directions, ascending and descending. Ascending practices, like the witness meditation I described earlier, involve disidentifying with body, mind, and world and feeling how everything can be embraced in one sound, taste, or experience; the many into one.

Descending practices involve experiencing the sacred in sensation, pleasure, and relationship, like Rachel was with her choir, until you can feel spirit equally in a grain of sand or the Milky Way; the one into many.

Non-dual practices engage ascending and descending activities with the increasing realization that both lead to the same non-dual awareness that emptiness and form are both manifestations of spirit.[13] This was happening as Rachel and Harry made love and culminated in a non-dual moment.

Attunement with self and others is spiritual practice.

In all the above examples, attunement led to a sense of the sacred. If the brain naturally moves toward freer flow of energy and more efficient and complex information processing, and if we are all connected (in some obvious and other mysterious ways), the natural direction of change is towards the unity of all consciousness, or oneness with spirit.

All spiritual traditions have principles and practices that they recommend as useful in living a life that is an expression of what's best in us. "Love your neighbor," the eight-fold path, and the twelve steps are all attempts to organize our thinking and behaving to be the best and truest we can be. Attunement, feeling courageously into ourselves and others and reaching for the most compassionate truth and action, supports all these practices. This naturally leads toward what Krishna (in the Bahadava Gita, speaking to the warrior Arjuna) called "karma yoga," having everything we think and do be an expression of God.[14]

1. Wilber (2003)

2. *Ibid*

3. Wilber (1995)

4. *Ibid*

5. Witt (2005)

6. Wilber (2003)

7. *Ibid*

8. *Ibid*

9. *Ibid*

10. *Ibid*

11. *Ibid*

12. *Ibid*

13. *Ibid*

14. Prabhavananda (1944)

14

Integration and Attunement

Daniel Siegal, in his lectures and books, offers neural integration as a definition of mental health and characterizes integration very specifically in the context of neural development, interpersonal functioning, and complex systems in general.[1] Integration involves differentiating and then connecting different elements in a complex system that is characterized by being open, energized, hierarchical, and capable of chaotic behavior, while not getting stuck in either rigidity or chaos. Human examples of complex systems demonstrating such integration are individual human brains and groups of people such as families, teams, tribes, villages, or nations.[2] An integrated system that does not get stuck in rigidity or lost in chaos tends to move toward more efficiency and greater complexity.[3]

I believe attunement naturally results in integration. When attuning to yourself, feeling compassionately inward with caring intent creates neural integration in the form of you becoming more flexible, adaptive, coherent, energized, and stable (FACES is the acronym Siegal, a self-professed "acronym addict," offers for this definition of integration).[4] You and me attuning to each other results in us creating what M. Scott Peck called "community."[5] Once again, that state is characterized by both of us becoming more flexible, adaptive, coherent, energized, and stable in service of some goal that is more important that either of us (the highest good).

At any given instant we are in various levels of attunement that support translating our sensory input, our implicit and explicit memories, our habits, our defensive systems, our anticipations of the future, and our conscious intent into our current functioning. These moments consecutively form a developmental trajectory where, in healthy development on any given developmental line (like our cognitive line, our moral line, our interpersonal line, or our psychosexual line), we tend to expand toward a larger sense of self and a wider embrace of the world, including and transcending different worldviews as we grow and mature.[6]If we suffer developmental arrest or distortion, we gather momentum toward being more rigid or chaotic.

You'll notice in all the therapy segments in this book, the transformative rhythm for individuals is identifying and clarifying some aspect of self and then compassionately incorporating that aspect into a larger self, and into a more coherent, caring self-narrative. Similarly, the rhythm for couples and families has been identifying and clarifying aspects of the individuals and systems, and then compassionately incorporating those aspects into more mature selves, and larger, more coherent and caring shared narratives.

I like to think of integration as a process that happens in individuals and groups if we don't get in its way. What slows integration? Critical judgment, overwhelming distress, rigid refusal to explore new perspectives and responses, and resistance to feeling into ourselves and others; in short, rigidity or chaos. What supports integration? Feeling compassionately into ourselves and others with caring intent; attunement.

Being great parents to our children.

As parents, it's our job to promote integration in our children. How do we do this? Give them a safe, caring environment and co-create secure attachments. Secure autonomous adults tend to create secure attachment with kids, and these adults have lives that make sense; coherent narratives characterized by self-reflection and a positive sense of past, present, and future.[7] How do secure autonomous adults create moments of secure attachment with kids? They are attuned.

Insecure attachment with kids is created by dismissive adults who are out of touch with their own emotions, preoccupied adults who are so distracted by intrusive associations, memories, or implicit learning that they are unable to create consistent contingent communication, and by unresolved, disorganized adults who are too terrified and/or terrifying to create consistent secure attachment.[8] How do such adults create a coherent narrative, heal past wounds, and learn to feel into their children? They learn to practice attunement with themselves and others.

Being great lovers with our spouse.

We all want to support integration, health, and joy in our spouse. How do we help our feminine partners bloom as open channels of emotion and wellsprings of love? How do we help our masculine partners thrive, be true to their deepest purpose, and be happy to be alive in the ongoing struggles of masculine existence?

Complex systems can move to more efficient organization as their parts are differentiated and then connected. All of us have a masculine aspect, a feminine aspect, and a deepest essence that is more masculine or feminine (especially in our lover relationships). Differentiation is understanding these different parts of ourselves, and integration is accepting and embracing these parts into a larger whole, dedicated to doing right by our emerging standards of what is beautiful, moral, and observably true.

Erotic polarity is at the heart of the ongoing love affair that continues throughout marriage. A masculine partner who knows this and regularly accesses his depth of understanding, humor, and shadow to open his feminine partner to deeper pleasure in life and love is supporting her integration as a woman. A feminine partner who accesses her erotic radiance, pleasure in the body, and current emotion to support her masculine partner's deepest purpose, and to draw him out of his worries, into his body, and then into her, is supporting his integration as a man.

All these goals are served by courageous attunement to ourselves and our spouse. As we feel into ourselves, we can discern what our masculine/feminine aspects are expressing and needing, and we can use that discernment to guide our caring intent. As we feel into our spouse, we can discern what his or her masculine/feminine aspects are expressing and needing, and we can use that discernment to help them be the best man, woman, lover, partner, parent, or friend they can be.

The attuned family

Research shows that, even though parents universally say their children make them happy, couples' happiness actually tends to diminish when the kids are in diapers, and are teenagers, and increases when they leave home.[9] Even though there are enormous stresses associated with these developmental periods in families, I believe this effect is partly due to pure ignorance. As I suggested in the river-rafting story, we feel we should know what to do in extreme situations, and sometimes we just don't.

I've found that understanding and practicing attunement in polarity, boundaries, violence, repair, developmental lines and levels, defensive states, states of healthy response, addiction, attachment, how our brains develop and function individually and interpersonally, spirituality, and many other areas helps prepare and guide us to being great parents and lovers.

My hope is that what you've explored and discovered in this book will help you be a more joyful man or woman, a more effective and confident parent, a more passionate, generous, and responsive lover, and more aware and able to create and sustain an attuned family through all the stresses and challenges that every family life cycle involves.

1. Siegal (2005)

2. *Ibid*

3. *Ibid*

4. *Ibid*

5. Peck (1987)

6. Wilber (2003)

7. Siegal (2005)

8. Siegal (1999)

9. Gilbert (2006)

References

Alexander, Charles N., and Langer, Ellen J. (1990). *Higher Stages of Human Development, Perspectives on Adult Growth.* New York: Oxford University Press

Bandura, Albert. (1973). *Aggression: a Social Learning Analysis.* Prentice-Hall

Beck, Don Edward, and Cowan, Christopher C. (1996). *Spiral Dynamics; mastering values, leadership, and change.* Malden, MA: Blackwell Publishing

Blum, Deborah. (2002). *Love at Goon Park.* Perseus Publishing

Bowlby, J. (1988). *A secure base: Parent-child attachment and healthy human development.* New York: Basic Books

Bowen, M. (1961). *Family Psychotherapy.* American Journal of Orthopsychiatry. 31: 40-60

Brizendine, Louann. (2006). *The Female Brain.* New York: Morgan Road Books

Cassidy, J., & Shaver, P. (Eds.). (1999), *Handbook of attachment: Theory, research, and clinical applications.* New York: Guilford Press

Cloniger, Robert C. (2004). *Feeling Good, the Science of Well-Being.* Oxford University Press

Cozolino, Louis J. (2002). *The Neuroscience of Psychotherapy.* New York: W.W. Norton & Co.

Deida, David. (2004). *Enlightened Sex.* Boulder, Colorado: Sounds True (audio recording)

---------. (1995). *Intimate Communion.* Deerfield Beach: Health Communications, Inc.

---------. (1997). *The Way of the Superior Man.* Austin: Plexus

Darwin, Charles. (1872). *The Expression of Emotions in Man and Animals.* London: John Murray

Dement, William C. and Vaughan, Christopher. (1999). *The Promise of Sleep.* New York: Dell

Erikson, Erik. (2000). *The Erik Erikson Reader.* Editor, Robert Coles: New York: W. W. Norton and Company, Inc

Fisher, Helen. (2004). *Why We Love: the Nature and Chemistry of Romantic Love.* New York: Henry Holt

Freud, Sigmund. (1949). *An Outline of Psycho-Analysis.* New York: W.W. Norton and Company.

Gelb, Michael J. (1988). *Present Yourself!* Torrance, Ca: Jalmar Press

Gilbert, Daniel. (2006). *Does Fatherhood Make You Happy?* New York: Time Magazine, June 19.

Gilligan, Carol. (1993). *In a Different Voice: Psychological Theory and Women's Development.* Cambridge, Mass.: Harvard University Press

Gilliland, B. E., & James, R. K. (1998). *Theories and strategies in counseling and psychotherapy.* Boston: Allyn & Bacon.

Giordano, Suzy. (2006). *Twelve Hours' Sleep by Twelve Weeks Old, a Step-by-Step Plan for Baby Sleep Success.* New York: Dutton

Gottman, John. (2005). Presented at a conference, *The Anatomy of Intimacy.* Foundation for the Contemporary Family, UC Irvine, November 5 and 6.

---------, (2001). *The Relationship Cure, a 5 Step Guide for Building Better Connections with Family, Friends, and Lovers.* New York: Crown Publishing

Hawkins, Jeff. (2000). *On Intelligence.* New York: Henry Holt and Company

Hayes, S.C., Strosahl, K., and Wilson, K. G. (1999) *Acceptance and Commitment Therapy: An Experimental Approach to Behavior Change.* New York: Guilford Press

Johnson, Susan. (2005). Presented at a conference, *The Anatomy of Intimacy*. Foundation for the Contemporary Family, UC Irvine, November 5 and 6.

Jung, Carl G. (1961) *Memories, Dreams, and Reflections*. New York: Random House

Kabat-Zinn, Jon. (2005). *Coming to Our Senses; healing ourselves and the world through mindfulness*. New York: Hyperion

Kahneman, Daniel. (1999). *Well-Being: Foundations of Hedonic Psychology*. Portland, Oregon: Book News, Inc.

Kegan, Robert. (1982) *The Evolving Self: Problme and Process in Humnan Development*. Cambridge, Mass: Harvard University Press

Lemonick, Michael D. (2004). *The Chemistry of Desire*. New York: Time Magazine, Jan. 19

----------. (2005). *The Bully Blight*. New York: Time Magazine, April 18

Levine, Judith. (2002). *Harmful to Minors*. Minneapolis: University of Mineapolis Press

Maslow, Abraham. (1962). *Toward a Psychology of Being*. Princeton, New Jersey: D. Van Nostrand Company, Inc.

McGoey, Peter F. (2006). *Surrender: An Oasis on the Path to Recovery*. California Association of Marriage and Family Therapists 2006 Annual Conferrence. Audio Recording. Garden Grove: Mdrecordings@aol.com

Minuchin, Salvador. (1974). *Families and Family Therapy*. Cambridge, Mass: Harvard University Press.

Ogden, Pat. (2006). Presented at a conference, *The Embodied Mind: Integration of the Body, Brain, and Mind in Cliical Practice*. UCLA, March 4 and 5

Peck, M. Scott (1987). *The Different Drum*. New York: Touchstone

Porges, S. W. (2006). Presented at a conference, *The Embodied Mind: Integration of the Body, Brain, and Mind in Clinical Practice*. UCLA, March 4 and 5

Prabhavananda, swami, and Isherwood, Christopher. (1944). *The Song of God: Bhagavad-Gita.* New York: The New American Library

Schnarch, David. (1997). *Passionate Marriage, Keeping Love and Intimacy Alive in Committed Relationships.* New York: Henry Holt and Company

Schore, Allan. (2006). Presented at a conference, *The Embodied Mind: Integration of the Body, Brain, and Mind in Clinical Practice.* UCLA, March 5

Siegal, Daniel J. (1999). *The Developing Mind.* New York: The Guilford Press

Siegal, Daniel J. and Hartzell, Mary. (2003). *Parenting from the Inside Out.* New York: Penguin

Siegal, Daniel J. (2005). *The Mindsight Lectures: cultivating insight and empathy in our internal and interpersonal lives.* Mind Your Brain, Inc.

Taylor, Shelley E. (2002). *The Tending Instinct: How Nurturing is Essential to Who We Are and How We Live.* New York: Henry Holt and Co.

Tolle, Eckhart. (1999). *The Power of Now.* Novato, Ca: New World

Tourneau, Melanie. (2001). *Pump Up to Cheer Up.* Psychology Today: May

van der Kolk, Bessel. (2005). Presented at a conference, *The Anatomy of Intimacy.* Foundation for the Contemporary Family. UC Irvine, Nov. 5 and 6.

Wilber, Ken. (2000). Sex, Ecology, Spirituality, the spirit of evolution. (1995). Boston: Shambhala Publications

---------. (2000). *Integral Psychology.* Boston and London: Shambala

---------. (2000). *A Brief History of Everything.* Boston: Shambala

---------. (2003). *Kosmic Consciousness.* Boulder: Sounds True (audio recording)

Wilson, Bill. (1939). *Big Book.* New York: Works Publishing Inc.

Wiseman, Richard. (2003). *The Luck Factor: Changing Your Luck, Changing Your Life: The Four Essential Principles.* Miramax

Witt, Keith. (2005) *Waking Up; Integrally Informed Individual and Conjoint Psychotherapy.* keithwitt@cox.net

978-0-595-43846-4
0-595-43846-6

Printed in the United States
119369LV00004BA/76/A